Google

Larry Cuban per Byrd

Leadership on the Line

Heifez

Saral

"Equity is the adaptive work."

Byrd
5D
4.1
45-76

ADAPTIVE CAPACITY

ADAPTIVE CAPACITY

How organizations can thrive in a **changing world**

Juan Carlos Eichholz
Foreword by Marty Linsky

LONDON   NEW YORK   SHANGHAI
MADRID   BARCELONA   BOGOTA
MEXICO CITY   MONTERREY   BUENOS AIRES

Published by
LID Publishing Inc.
420 Round Hill Road
Greenwich, CT 06831
info@lidpublishing.com
www.lidpublishing.com

A member of:

BPR
Business Publishers Roundtable
www.businesspublishersroundtable.com

© Juan Carlos Eichholz 2014
© LID Publishing Inc. 2014

Printed in the United States
ISBN: 978-0-9852864-8-4

Cover and page designer: Armen Edgarian
Copyeditor: Erin Clermont
Proofreader: Debra Rhoades
Indexer: Nancy Kopper

To Catalina

CONTENTS

PART TWO: HOW TO INCREASE AN ORGANIZATION'S ADAPTIVE CAPACITY

CHAPTER 4
PURPOSE: THE ORGANIZATION'S SOUL   119

CHAPTER 5
STRATEGY: THE ORGANIZATION'S BRAIN   135

FOREWORD

This book has been written at the right time. Fifteen years ago it would not have resonated with senior executives, most of whom were experiencing good times they thought were going to last and last and last. A few years from now it will be too late for many who would benefit from it, perhaps you among them.

It was not so long ago that many smart people believed that the world was in the early stages of what Peter Schwartz and his colleagues called "The Long Boom" in their book of that title first published in 1999. Prosperity forever.

In 2002, when Juan Carlos Eichholz and our other colleagues opened the doors of Cambridge Leadership Associates (CLA), our global consulting firm, potential clients were not interested in adaptation. At most, they wanted advice on how to go not from Good to Great, in Jim Collins' memorable phrase, but from Greater to Even Greater.

Hah. Looks pretty shortsighted with the benefit of hindsight.

All of that changed in 2007. The economic downturn was more than just a "correction," as my financial advisor likes to call it whenever the stock market tanks, our family nest egg shrivels, and it begins to look, again, as if I will have to die with my work boots on. The moment was a fundamental reset in the way most people looked at the world. Reality set in. Life would never be the same.

Look, I grew up in the 1940s and 1950s. The pace of change was slow and steady, easy to accommodate. I remember watching television for the first time in 1949, on a tiny snowy screen on a clear, crisp November day in the basement of my best friend's house. It was a football game, the annual meeting of the United States Military Academy and the United States Naval Academy, the Army-Navy game. I was glued to the set, although I could barely make out the players. Then came my own family's little TV, replacing our huge radio console, then a bigger TV, then color. Step by step, over a decade or more we easily accommodated the incremental additions to our home entertainment resources. Those were pleasant years of welcome change at a comfortable pace. True, our family was not what you would call early adopters.

How different is the world we live in now. We are inundated with confusing and inconclusive data; endure rapid, significant change as a constant; and cope under conditions of great uncertainty, ambiguity, and unknown futures.

It is into this environment that this book steps, creating some much-needed clarity and order around how to understand and thrive under these new conditions.

Saying all that, that this is the right book for all senior executives in the times in which we live, oh how I wish I had it on my bedside reading table nearly forty years ago when I took my first management job. (Of course, that bedside table reference is just a metaphor for what I *should* be reading. There are eleven business-oriented books on my bedside table right now that are mostly collecting dust while I divert myself nightly with lighter reading that helps me get my dotage-required eight hours of sleep.)

That first management job was as editor of a weekly alternative newspaper that had been purchased by friends from the '60s-style cooperative that had founded it several years before. The new owners and I were trying to move the publication from an underfinanced, worker-subsidized, albeit very culturally hip and politically outside publication with a narrow but fervent, mostly young following to a more mainstream but still hip, high-quality, politically engaged but less predictable alternative to the traditional media, reaching a much wider readership, and leading to a financially stable if not significantly profitable business.

It was a huge adaptive challenge, although I was at least twenty years away from having the language to describe it that way, and having read this book, now realize I was another twenty years away from having the diagnostic and implementation tools to meet that challenge in a systematic and systemic way. Where was Juan Carlos when I needed him?

I operated intuitively, made every possible mistake leading the change, most of them more than once, and barely comprehended what I was trying to do. In Eichholz's terms, the newspaper was a communal and action-driven organization, organized as a cooperative, but needing to put out a product every week, week after week. We needed to move into being more innovative, and yes, more bureaucratic, to establish systems in order not to operate only under survival-driven sustained chaos. I put my head down and charged ahead, meeting resistance at every turn, and for the first couple of years at least, made no progress at all. Boy, did I need what this book offers.

What is in these pages is a gift to you.

First, there is language to help you diagnose the situation you are in. What kind of organization are you helping to manage? What are its qualities along the communal-bureaucratic-action-driven-innovation dimensions, and where do you need to move it? What are the state of the external environment, the current reality in the industry you are in or planning to enter, and the best assumptions about where it is going in the future?

Juan Carlos Eichholz offers us a set of frameworks and tools to help us get there. What are the levers in your organization that you can use to make progress? What is the difference between what was required for progress in the tranquil time in which I came of age, during the years of unbridled growth, and what is required now? How do you adjust your purpose, strategy, structure, culture, and talent to increase the adaptive capacity of your organization as a whole and the individuals within it?

Those potential clients we talk with post-2007 are no longer focused on going from Great to Greater. Their attention is on how they can create organizations that can survive and thrive under conditions of internal and external uncertainty they've never experienced before. They know that the skills and experience that got them where they are will not get them or their organization to the next place. They are aware that the emphasis on execution that has driven them for so long, which has become part of their identity and core skill-set and that of their teams, now must be tempered with a new set of insights, capacities, and techniques all centered on developing their own and their organization's adaptive capacity. It is the capacity to adapt, as Darwin first noted, that will separate the winners from the losers as far ahead as we can see.

As Eichholz says succinctly, "Instead of concentrating on becoming very good at doing any one particular thing, companies should concentrate on becoming very good at learning how to do new things." Eichholz generously acknowledges that he is building on the work of others. Adaptive Leadership is not a new idea. However, by bringing those foundational ideas to an organizational setting and developing new frameworks and tools for analysis and action, he has charted new territory and created new knowledge.

As I write this, I am serving on the boards of two organizations: a fast-growing start-up and a well-established educational institution drifting into deep decline. I have used the frameworks offered here to diagnose where these organizations are and where they need to move. I have a sense of which levers need to be adjusted to enable each to increase its adaptive capacity and enhance its potential for being successful down the road. My colleagues on those boards and the senior managers we oversee had better watch out. I am on a tear.

This book has been a gift to me as well.

Marty Linsky

Co-Founder and Principal, Cambridge Leadership Associates (CLA)
Faculty, Harvard Kennedy School
New York
April 2014

PROLOGUE: THE TREES

In May 2005 *Fortune* magazine published a cover story by reporter Fred Vogelstein titled "Gates vs. Google: Why Google Scares Bill Gates." At the time, the search engine company founded by twenty-somethings Sergey Brin and Larry Page was just a fraction of the Internet powerhouse it would become, and Gates' Microsoft was still the sole dominant player in the world of PC software. The article begins with an extraordinary anecdote describing the moment in December 2003 when the enormous scope of Google's challenge to Microsoft first became clear to Gates. He had taken a look at descriptions for open jobs at Google on the company website and noticed they were looking for engineers with backgrounds that had nothing to do with a web search business but were identical to Microsoft job specs. Gates later that day sent an email to some of his executives saying, in effect, "We have to watch these guys. It looks like they are building something to compete with us."[1]

I recall reading the article when it was published and being impressed that Bill Gates would devote his time to analyzing descriptions of Google's open jobs. As a business consultant and a professor of leadership and organizational change, I was fascinated learning that the founder and CEO of one of the largest corporations in the world would resort to such unconventional means to better understand the evolution of his industry and the opportunities and threats confronting Microsoft.

Perhaps Gates had learned the importance of observing as many signals as possible in part through his failure to do so a decade earlier. When the Internet was in its initial steps of massive development and penetration, Microsoft bet against it, mainly because Gates believed it had little potential. Fortunately for the company, that view was soon challenged by other executives who forced a change in Microsoft's strategy and successfully mobilized sufficient resources to seize an Internet foothold.

Although Microsoft was able to adapt quickly enough in the 1990s to keep its prominent position in the information technology industry, it was unable to repeat the process in the 2000s. Not only was Microsoft incapable of challenging Google's core search engine business despite huge investments in the effort, but the company also saw its own core business as a software developer decline over time, especially when Apple's new devices changed the playing field.

Why did Microsoft fail to adapt to the changing world of technology, despite its founder's prescient recognition of the threat posed by the likes of Google? How could the outcome have been changed? And will Microsoft be able to reinvent itself in the years to come, thereby ensuring its continued existence and perhaps a rebound to the pinnacle of business success?

forest metaphor

These questions have no clear answers, but one thing is sure: predicting the future and acting intelligently on one's forecast has become an increasingly difficult — and risky — task. There are so many trees out there in the dynamic world we live in, all very different from each other and each growing in its own tangled, impenetrable thicket, that mapping the forest and making sense of its byways is now harder than ever.

For that very reason, the ability to remain competitive in this changing world depends less on an organization's capacity to predict the future than on its capacity to adapt to that future as fast as possible. Microsoft's decline can be traced to the fact that its *adaptive capacity* fell over time — or at least did not increase quickly enough to match its competitors. So even though looking outside to understand the trends that will affect your organization is certainly important, looking inside to diagnose your ability to adapt to the impending changes is equally important. It is also extremely difficult. As the world gets more complex, so do organizations, and their own internal forests become more and more difficult to discern among the trees.

Book's Purpose:

The purpose of this book is to help top executives look inside their own organizations, make sense of the forest growing there, and understand how the trees may need to be nurtured, pruned, replanted, or felled to create a more adaptive organism. Having worked closely with executives of large corporations with the goal of making progress on their toughest organizational challenges, I have learned a lot about carrying out changes that can improve the organization's performance in a sustainable way. At the same time, I've realized how difficult it can be for executives to see the big picture where their own company is concerned and do the necessary adaptive work.

Most successful executives are very good at understanding the business they are in and visualizing the opportunities in front of them. However, they tend to falter when trying to mobilize the organization to take advantage of those opportunities. The typical business executive behaves like an auto racer who tries to drive faster simply by flooring the accelerator; he or she fails to recognize that the engine may need a tune-up or even a complete overhaul if the car is to achieve its full potential.

Making matters worse, unlike auto racers, who work with teams of mechanics to keep their vehicles in tip-top shape, most business executives have to figure out on their own how to mobilize their organizations to be more adaptive. In fact, this is one of their most important responsibilities in the knowledge era, when an organization's success depends less on the talent of the CEO than on unleashing the potential of employees. Unfortunately, maximizing this potential is generally a process of trial and error, given both the inherent complexity of the task and the current stage of theoretical development of this field.

This book is intended to represent a step forward on our journey toward understanding adaptation at the organizational level, especially from the perspective of top executives and their needs. It is certainly neither the first nor the final word on the subject. Specifically, it builds on the ideas about adaptive leadership initially developed by Harvard professor Ronald Heifetz and Riley Sinder. I first met Heifetz as a graduate student in the mid-1990s. His book *Leadership Without Easy Answers* is a vital reference point for understanding leadership and authority in the context of adaptive change. It was later supplemented by the more practical and personal book *Leadership on the Line*, co-authored by Heifetz with Harvard professor Marty Linsky. The application of these ideas to the development of leadership capacity in organizations through Cambridge Leadership Associates (CLA), the consulting firm founded by Heifetz and Linsky in 2002, allowed them to further advance the depth and breadth of their framework, culminating in the publication of *The Practice of Adaptive Leadership*, by Heifetz, Linsky, and Alexander Grashow, senior advisor and former CEO of CLA.[2]

In my role as a professor at Adolfo Ibáñez Business School in Chile, the founder and director of the Adaptive Leadership Center, and the driver of CLA's practice in Latin America, I have partnered with Heifetz, Linsky, and Grashow for a decade, teaching, consulting with corporations, and conducting various workshops and learning experiences together. *Adaptive Capacity* is the product of what I have learned in collaboration with many others who are part of a larger community of professors and practitioners that help organizations tackle change processes with an adaptive approach.

Part One describes the broad concepts of change, adaptation, and organizational complexity that underlie our approach. Part Two moves on to examine specific practical techniques that top executives can apply to increase their organizations' adaptive capacity, including a number of variations demanded by companies facing different kinds of internal and external challenges.

You may be tempted to jump immediately into Part Two, particularly if you are a business executive facing pressing challenges that demand swift action. However, I urge you to invest some time in reading Part One first. Increasing your organization's adaptive capacity is not just a matter of looking at a set of variables and trying to modify them. It would be difficult and probably ineffective to do so without understanding why adaptive capacity is important. This is the question addressed in Chapter 1, "Everything Starts with a Problem," which analyzes why organizations tend to remain in equilibrium and how that can be changed, which in turn requires a sophisticated overview of human nature in both its individual and its systemic aspects.

Furthermore, if you hope to make your organization more adaptive, it's essential to comprehend what an adaptive organization is really like, which is the focus of Chapter 2, "Organizations Face Problems Differently." Here I explain how adaptive capacity may need to vary from one kind of business to another. Google, for example, needs a very different adaptive capacity than a company like BHP Billiton, one of the largest mining companies in the world. Consider the fact that when executives at Google talk about "long-term planning" they are probably thinking about the next three years, whereas senior managers at BHP Billiton use the same phrase to describe strategies for the next thirty years. This single contrast suggests the differences these two companies should be expected to have — and actually do have — in their decision-making styles, structures, levels of disequilibrium, process definitions, turnover rates, and many other aspects. Nonetheless, both companies can be more adaptive within the framework of their own realities. To make sense of those different realities, I discuss four kinds of organizations, each requiring different levels of adaptive capacity: action-driven, bureaucratic, communal, and innovative.

It's not enough, though, to have a good diagnosis of your organization's adaptive capacity and the gaps that may need to be addressed. Chapter 3, "The Problem as an Adaptive Challenge," will help you understand how to design and conduct a process aimed at increasing that adaptive capacity as a way of better tackling the business challenges that are putting pressure on the company.

Equipped with the concepts outlined in Part One, you'll be prepared to turn to Part Two, where we'll examine a number of variables that, if consciously worked through, may trigger an increase in your own organization's adaptive capacity. Each of the five chapters in Part Two will analyze one of the key dimensions of an organization, examining the variables that can affect your ability to unleash your people's capabilities. These dimensions, which together form the organic whole that makes up your organization, are:

- Purpose — the organization's soul
- Strategy — the organization's brain
- Structure — the organization's skeleton
- Culture — the organization's blood
- Talent — the organization's heart

At the end of the book, you should be prepared to answer these four questions about your organization, which can also be applied to your team or even to yourself:

- How much adaptive capacity does it have?
- Is that adaptive capacity enough to meet the challenges it faces?
- How can its adaptive capacity be increased?
- What are the variables that may increase its adaptive capacity?

I suggest you consider these questions carefully now and refer to them often as you read the chapters that follow. They serve as guideposts throughout the journey we are about to start.

PART ONE

WHAT IS
ADAPTIVE CAPACITY?

Nearly a century and a half ago, the great biologist Charles Darwin revolution-
ized the study of life on Earth with his theory of evolution through variation and
natural selection. His theory can be summed up in his famous line: "It is not the
strongest of the species that survives, nor the most intelligent that survives. It is
the one that is the most adaptable to change."[3]

Darwin's idea applies not only to biological evolution but also to social
evolution — especially in today's organizational world, where increasing
levels of external change demand increasing levels of internal adaptation.

In biology, adaptation is a natural process that organisms engage in unconsciously. By contrast, organizational adaptation is hard work; indeed, it is so *conscious*
psychologically and socially difficult and challenging that it may even become *process*
dangerous for those who promote it because of the resistance it generates. It
is also purposeful work, which should be strategically designed and led with
specific changes and goals in mind.

These ideas are the basis of Part One of this book, which addresses the
following issues:

- What is organizational adaptation?
- What are the implications of the current economic, social, and business
  environments for organizational adaptive capacity?
- Why is organizational adaptation often painful and fiercely resisted
  by members of the organization?
- What is the role of authorities in making adaptation happen?
- How does adaptive capacity vary depending on the nature of the
  organization and the environment in which it operates?
- What must companies do to manage the process of adaptation effectively?

CHAPTER 1

EVERYTHING STARTS WITH A PROBLEM

If there weren't a problem, adaptation wouldn't be necessary. People and organizations thrive when they face problems successfully. And when they avoid problems, they may not survive.

David Franco was born with a newspaper in his hands.[4] The first son of the founder of a local newspaper called the *Home Star*, he was introduced to the business at a young age. It was the early 1960s, and after school he would go to his father's office and hear him talking on the phone with prominent newsmakers in their small city and then take part in the meeting at which the headlines for next day were decided; he might also help choose a photo for the front page or distribute newspapers at night, and always talk with his father about politics while driving back home.

Over the years, David learned every single aspect of the business and every single person who worked at the firm, most of whom had been there for quite a long time. Before graduating from high school, he knew how to conduct an interview, write an article, conduct editorial discussions with journalists, sell ads to clients, work the printing equipment, and drive a truck to distribute the newspapers at three in the morning. His father had taught him everything about the newspaper, and David was passionate about it.

Everybody knew that at some point David would take over the firm. But it happened much sooner than expected. While David was at college, his father had a fatal heart attack, which caused David to drop out and replace his father in the business. As sad and unexpected as the situation was, David faced the enormous challenge before him with determination and resolution, relying on the support of his mother and siblings as well as the collaboration and advice of the employees. Little by little, David became more empowered, and actually navigated the initial years quite well, avoiding the crisis that a small organization like this one could face in the sudden absence of its founder.

As soon as he felt the situation was stable enough, David began putting all his energy, creativeness, and know-how into making the *Home Star* grow and compete directly with other local media. He worked with the people who had been loyal to his father, and with others he brought into the firm, giving the newspaper a fresh new look and a new emphasis on investigative journalism that would dig deeply into important issues. It didn't take long for David to gain the respect of his employees and to become well known in the local industry. In his mid-thirties, with the experience he had gained and his willingness to experiment, David added new sections, magazines, and supplements to the newspaper and launched a project to increase subscriptions, doubling the circulation in a few years. He knew more than anyone else in the firm about the business, was on top of everything, involved in every decision, working hard, inspiring and taking care of people. The results were encouraging.

When the '90s arrived, the *Home Star* had become the main local newspaper, and everything was under control. But David wanted to go further in the emerging globalized world in which media integration was becoming a significant trend. He decided to buy a radio station and a newspaper in a nearby larger city. It was a big step to take, and it felt like a good strategic decision.

As he had done when his father passed away, David faced this new challenge by fully involving himself in both acquired businesses. He moved to the nearby city and assumed the main management role, which would allow him to be on top of everything, make the decisions, get to know the people, and understand every detail of how the firms functioned. It had worked before; it should work now.

But it didn't. Instead, some unexpected things started happening.

A couple of months after his arrival, some key people resigned at both the radio station and the newspaper. David was a bit surprised by these events but didn't ascribe too much importance to them. On the contrary, he put more energy into making the new businesses work well, just as he had done for more than two decades in his hometown business. Yet he increasingly felt as if things were not working properly. It was as if people didn't understand that the reality of the business had changed — that a new owner had taken over, that the rhythm of the industry had accelerated, and that growth was essential for survival in a world being reshaped by globalization and new technologies. Despite David's efforts to convey this message, his employees continued doing things in their own way, causing David to become increasingly frustrated and worried.

Moreover, things started deteriorating at David's beloved *Home Star*. Employees resented that David was not there as he used to be, that decisions could not be made without him, that commercial clients wanted to meet him, that reporters no longer had access to the inside information David used to provide. David couldn't understand this: "I have problems all over, both where I am and where I am not. What's going on with my people?"

Most surprising of all, the same traits and behaviors that had enabled David Franco to achieve such success in the wake of his father's passing were now having the opposite effects. The *Home Star* had become too dependent on him and at the same time he had taken charge of two organizations that were not used to being conducted in such a directive way, with a boss who would micromanage and make all decisions. Even worse, because of the combined size of the three businesses and the changes that were starting to take place in the industry, there was no possibility that David could be on top of everything. Now in his mid-forties, he felt overwhelmed, tired, and disappointed by the results he was obtaining, despite the enormous effort he'd put in in the last three years.

David had a problem. And though he didn't see it that way, he was an important part of the problem. He had become the bottleneck of his own big organization, and if he didn't adapt, things would surely get worse. But that adaptation would not be easy for him. In order to empower people who would allow the organization to grow and adapt to a rapidly changing industry, he would have to be less involved in day-to-day operations and devote more time to having conversations with his employees. He would have to ask more questions and give fewer instructions, avoid making every decision, accept mistakes, and, most of all, learn to work without knowing and being in control of every single detail.

This was easy to say, but difficult to carry out. In order to allow his organization to continue thriving, David had to change the recipe he had learned from his father, which had worked for him for so many years. He had to stop doing many of the things he was so passionate about. He might have to fire some of his — and his father's — longtime collaborators at home, who were used to a paternalistic style and unable to take responsibility. The very survival of the organization — at least under his ownership — might be at stake, hanging on the owner's adaptive capacity.

The firm needed to function in a different way if it was to overcome the problem it was in, but that could only happen if its owner and top executive changed himself.

CARLY FIORINA, HP, AND THE DIFFICULTIES OF ADAPTATION

When Carly Fiorina was appointed CEO of HP in 1999, the board of directors gave her a fundamental mission: "Totally re-create and reinvent HP according to the original HP Way."[5] It was clear that the company had a problem, but how did Fiorina interpret this somewhat contradictory mandate? "Preserve the best, reinvent the rest," as she used to say. And that is what she did, or tried to do.

A powerful and determined woman with a strong reputation in America's corporate world, Fiorina sought to transform the bureaucratic company that HP had become during the previous decade into the leading actor in electronic services, accelerating change and risk-taking in the same way she had successfully done as president of the global service provider Lucent, an equipment and technology spinoff of AT&T.

The members of HP's board understood that Hewlett-Packard was no longer the innovative and admired technological company it had been since its founding in 1939. This sense of urgency led them to select Fiorina, the first CEO in HP's history to come from outside, to be a woman, to be under forty-five, and to come from a non-engineering background. Moreover, she became the first woman to lead a Fortune 20 company. The board clearly wanted a change; a survey among HP's top 300 executives showed in 1997 that they wanted a shift toward more creative thinking and more customer focus.[6] But they wanted this change to reflect the "HP Way," a long tradition of doing things according to certain values that had been embodied and cultivated for years by the two founders, one of whom, emeritus board member William Hewlett, was still alive when Fiorina took over.

Being a marketer, Fiorina started by refreshing some old-fashioned symbols of the company, giving credit to everything that had been done before, but trying to give the old symbols a new twist. She renewed the classic "rules of the garage" that represented the company's soul, and changed not only the logo's shape but also the text it contained, using the initials *HP* instead of Hewlett-Packard.

These symbolic changes were accompanied by an organizational restructuring that divided the company into six divisions and reduced the number of product groups from 87 to 12. Fiorina also implemented a decision that had been made by the board before her arrival: she separated the company's technical equipment division into the stand-alone Agilent Technologies. The core strategy, which Fiorina made a special effort to communicate aggressively throughout the organization, was a simple one: to position HP for the Internet's second wave, creating new e-services and the hardware and software to deliver them. But the new strategy and the structural changes led to layoffs, which many longtime HP employees deeply resented.

Fiorina knew that within the company she still had many of the best engineers and that HP boasted a long history of technological innovation. But she also knew that this was not enough to compete in an industry that had many strong players and was changing dramatically. She therefore also looked for opportunities outside. She attempted to acquire PricewaterhouseCoopers' global management and information technology consulting business, which would have meant integrating 31,000 new employees despite the layoffs that were taking place because of the restructuring and the economic downturn. By the end of 2000 she had to back off, giving in to internal resistance to the acquisition, the same thing that had happened with her attempt to acquire the computer-services business EDS, also highly resisted by the shareholders.

Nonetheless, Fiorina did not give up in her efforts to make HP grow beyond its internal capacities. In 2001, she went for a deal that would become her most relevant challenge — and a personal battle: the merger with Compaq, a leading competitor in the PC industry. The announcement of the merger, after months of secret negotiations, produced an immediate negative reaction among analysts on Wall Street. More important, it created a conflict within the board and a division among shareholders, with strong opposition to the proposal coming from the Hewlett and Packard heirs, led by Walter Hewlett himself. After six months of a hard and open dispute, the shareholders voted in favor of the merger by a margin of only 2.8 percent. Fiorina's victory was accompanied by a lingering sense of distrust, wounded egos, and loss. Many people saw in this the final burial of the famous and traditional HP Way.

As one executive put it: "We were looking for a CEO who would shake up a company that had grown slow and stale. The moral of the story: watch out what you wish for, because you may get it!"[7]

If HP had a problem before Fiorina arrived, many people now thought that she was the problem. Her reputation was damaged, thousands of employees had been laid off, and the stock price had fallen during her tenure. Finally, in early 2005, amid press reports that the board was considering a new restructuring plan that would limit Fiorina's power, she entered a board meeting and, without expecting it or receiving any explanation, was fired.

To this day, observers differ in their interpretations of Fiorina's performance both in terms of the strategy she followed and in the way she implemented it. The fact is that after she left, HP's stock started rising (a trend that continued for the next three years) and the company regained its position as the world's number one PC manufacturer and one of the top innovator companies.

Were these positive developments due to Carly Fiorina? Could the changes she made have been implemented with less pain? Were they sustainable? Was Fiorina's firing necessary? And in the years to come, how open would the new HP be to further strategic changes?

Questions like these have arisen in the histories of countless companies disrupted by the turmoil of change. Whenever significant change is undertaken, some sort of resistance should be expected from particular factions or groups within an organization, even when it is generally conceded that the change is good and necessary. This is because, despite the benefits that will come from change, there will typically be costs that few or several employees will have to bear. For this reason, the HP story of painful acceptance of change is one we'll see repeated again and again in one industry after another.

Resistance to change is nothing new. Back in 1513, pioneering political scientist Niccolò Machiavelli wrote about it in his masterpiece, *The Prince*:

> It must be remembered that there is nothing more difficult to plan, more doubtful of success, nor more dangerous to manage than a new system. For the initiator has the enmity of all who would profit by the preservation of the old institution and merely lukewarm defenders in those who gain by the new one. The hesitation of the latter arises in part from the fear of their adversaries, who have the laws on their side, and in part from the general skepticism of mankind, which does not really believe in an innovation until experience proves its value.[8]

Good Point

In the case of HP, resistance arose from the middle and lower levels of the organization when an executive from the top, Fiorina, attempted to impose change. In other cases, resistance arises from the top executive himself, as in the case of David Franco, for example, who had to personally change for the organization he had built to succeed in the future.

EQUILIBRIUM, DISEQUILIBRIUM, AND ADAPTIVE CAPACITY

The *Home Star* and HP had problems that demanded organizational and strategic change. The sources and the magnitude of the problems were very different, but their fundamental nature was the same. It was not just a matter of making a decision and leaping into action. To make change happen, a reframing process had to take place in many shareholders' and employees' mentalities and behaviors, which in turn were connected to assumptions, values, loyalties, attitudes, competencies, and habits that needed to be questioned. This is the process we call *adaptive change*. It has little do to with rationality or making the right decision. Instead, it is closely tied to many other factors, including human emotions that tend to prevent change or make it too difficult or slow, despite the pressing need for change.

Definition

David Franco had to fight against himself if he wanted to effectively face the problems that his organization was experiencing. Yet why should he change a style of managing the *Home Star* when it had been successful for more than two decades? Moreover, he had learned this style from his own father, whose image and lessons were still resonating in David's head. Would he have enough adaptive capacity to question himself, to act in ways he was not used to and didn't feel comfortable with, to confront his oldest collaborators and push them to change themselves?

At HP, Carly Fiorina met resistance to her efforts to transform the organization because there were values at stake connected to what many people in the company thought of as the company's identity. This identity was built on the company's culture — the HP Way — and the legacy of its two founders, William Hewlett and David Packard. Fiorina knew this and actually made attempts to honor that legacy, but not sufficiently, not in a strategic way. Her efforts faltered because of her failure to recognize that HP's adaptive capacity was not large enough to enable the company to go where Fiorina wanted to take it — at the pace she wanted and with the type of managerial style she embodied.

Of course, the *Home Star* and HP aren't the only companies faced with changing environments that pose major challenges. It's difficult to think of any kind of organization that has not been touched by the many rapid changes that are currently revolutionizing the world of business and demanding unprecedented levels of adaptive capability from companies that want to survive and thrive.

Think, for example, of the record companies that tried to adapt to technological change by fighting against the many music-sharing websites that emerged in the late 1990s and early 2000s. While they were devoting their energy to lawsuits in a vain attempt to stop piracy and copyright violations — trying desperately to protect and then to restore the previous status quo — Apple came up with the iPod, transforming the music industry and creating a new status quo in which the record companies had little role to play.

Or consider companies that extract resources like oil, gas, coal, and minerals from the earth. They now have to deal with more empowered communities, not only in developed countries but in the developing world, which are increasingly unwilling to put up with the environmental damage extractive industries cause in exchange for the relatively poor-paying jobs they create. How can these businesses adapt to the new realities in a way that will create increasing value to everyone?

Nor is the challenge of adaptation restricted to business. Nonprofit organizations and governments are in trouble, too, confronting problems they do not understand, under pressure to provide fast solutions they do not have at hand to people who have higher expectations than ever before, and all this within a political climate that is more inclined to polarization than cooperation. How can such once-respected sectors of society as government, education, religion, and health care regain the sense of public trust and confidence they once commanded? This is a major adaptive challenge that may even suggest the need to reframe the social contract under which we've lived for more than two centuries in the Western world.

These cases and situations, and many others we will visit in this book, show the importance of increasing a person's and an organization's adaptive capacity in times that demand change.

Of course, in some circumstances companies can survive and even thrive for a time without developing any significant adaptive capacity. When the environment is calm and the organization is in a state of equilibrium, adaptation may not be necessary. In this condition, simply "keeping on doing the same things we've always done" may not be a bad strategy at all. In fact, when people know what they have to do in order to get the expected results, good management becomes a matter of managing the resources at hand and allocating them wisely rather than changing things for the sake of change. As the saying goes, "If it's not broken, don't fix it!"

A situation like this, in which equilibrium allows successful management without the need for adaptation, is a comfortable one. No wonder many executives want to believe they and their organizations exist in a state of equilibrium even when it is not true. It's a soothing belief and therefore an attractive one.

But even when equilibrium really exists, we see that today's world does not allow most organizations to stay in that comfortable situation for long. In a world of sweeping, rapid change, it's likely that what works today will no longer work in the near future. Equilibrium is likely to be replaced by disequilibrium — and probably sooner than you expect.

Disequilibrium comes from a wide variety of sources, and when that happens, an adaptive challenge is faced; that is, the organization must look for new ways of doing certain things, battling against the natural tendency to resist the need for change.

Think of what happens when a new competitor comes into the game, or when there is an economic downturn, or when growth demands overseas expansion, or when a merger takes place, or when it becomes difficult to attract talent, or when key industry regulations are changed, or when local communities protest business practices, or when a new generation comes into the workforce. Or what happens when a new CEO is appointed, or when the team members stop getting along, or when workers feel overwhelmed and purpose is lost, or when there is a conflict among partners, or when a disruptive new technology is introduced, or when an organizational restructuring takes place.

All these problems, and many more, pose adaptive challenges for a company, meaning that it is not possible to continue thinking and acting in the exact same way people are used to. When such problems arise, a certain level of tension is felt as a consequence of the disequilibrium the problems create. But organizations react in different manners to these stimuli. Some see them as challenges, taking advantage of them and thriving through an adaptive process, faster or slower, more or less effectively; some look for ways to avoid hearing the message and try to restore the previous equilibrium; and some deceive themselves, thinking that they are adapting when they are really doing the same things as in the past but with a different wrapping.

Why these differences? They arise because, as we've already seen, the adaptive capacity of those companies is not the same: some are more adaptive than others. Having a greater adaptive capacity allows an organization to turn problems into challenges and to adapt successfully easier and faster. The deeper challenge, therefore, is to find ways to increase the adaptive capacity before the occurrence of stimuli that generate imbalance.

One way companies do this is by deliberately avoiding a state of equilibrium, or creating a state of disequilibrium before it is created by external conditions. As Bill Gates used to say to his people, "Microsoft is always two years away from failure," meaning that they had to permanently challenge themselves in order to remain in business.[9] Hence some business managers have repurposed the old slogan as "If it isn't broken, break it!" By deliberately creating disruptive change, these managers strive to avoid the risk of complacency that can arise when a long period of equilibrium lulls an

[margin note: possible change factors:]

[margin note: ways organizations react:]

[margin note: One way to build adaptive capacity:]

organization's members and blunts the sharp edge of adaptive capacity they'll need sooner or later. It looks like an extreme approach to the challenge of improving your adaptive capacity and one that may not be necessary if you follow the advice presented in Part Two of this book.

TECHNICAL WORK, ADAPTIVE WORK, AND AVOIDANCE

The central theme of this book is the importance of adaptive capacity for sustainable business success, but adaptation is not the only important task that executives must perform. Another type of work, which we call *technical work*, must also be performed, and performed well. The difference between adaptive work and technical work lies in the idea of learning — that is, knowing whether new assumptions, values, loyalties, attitudes, competencies or habits are required to carry out the work ahead.

If your existing business plan is enough to tackle the challenges you currently face, it will just be a matter of applying the know-how already at the company's disposal, and that is technical work. It may be routine work, for which protocols and systems exist; or it may be something that goes beyond routine that can be solved by applying existing knowledge within the firm or expert knowledge that can be outsourced. If that is not the case, and learning becomes necessary, you are in the domain of adaptive work.

An important part of HP's work as it strives to secure and strengthen its position in the world of digital technology is in fact technical— building and distributing the third series of the Pavilion laptop in those days, for example. The same applies to the *Home Star*, which must manage technical work processes such as producing clear, well-edited copy to fill its news columns and running its printing equipment at peak efficiency.

On the other hand, how technical is carrying out the merger with Compaq or buying and running a radio station or a newspaper larger than yours? Top executives at HP may well had experience in acquisitions, and they could hire a good consulting firm to help them manage such details as the integration of different information technology systems for managing payroll and inventory controls. But when a merger occurs, a lot of learning needs to take place in thousands of employees from both companies, regarding such issues as loyalties, organizational values and behaviors, status and power affairs, practices and protocols, just to name a few. Similarly, David Franco and the members of his team had a lot to learn after expanding their company to include media outlets in a new city — especially during a time of dramatic change in the media business.

Because these situations that demand learning arise more often and at a faster pace in today's world than ever before, adaptive work is steadily becoming a greater aspect of people's and companies' lives. But the tricky thing is that people, especially top executives, tend to treat the adaptive challenges they face through technical work instead of adaptive work.

Why does this happen? It happens because we have a natural tendency to rely on what we already know and control, well expressed in that old saying, "When you have a hammer, everything looks like a nail." What is the effect of doing this? The result is that the adaptive challenge is not really faced but avoided, even though all people involved are acting in good faith, trusting that they are doing what they have to do. This is what happened when Carly Fiorina put so much focus and effort into the macro work — investing in the brand, acquiring companies, restructuring, and inspiring people — and put so little into the micro work — building alliances, pacing the work, hearing the different voices, acknowledging people's losses, and managing their distress. The macro work involved tasks she'd already performed successfully at Lucent and was very capable of handling at HP; the micro work was much more novel and difficult, which made it tempting and easy for her to minimize its importance and ultimately neglect it.

Technical work is very different from adaptive work, indeed. Where in one there are clear answers and little uncertainty, in the other there are no clear answers and uncertainty can be very high. Where one involves no big choices, the other involves difficult choices and, therefore, losses. Where one is straightforward and is executed through precise instructions, the other is time-consuming and demands a lot of conversation and renegotiation of loyalties and power relations.

Where one calls for people's hands, feet, and mouths, the other calls for people's brains, hearts, eyes, and ears. Where one is focused on the task, the other is focused on the people connected to the task. Where one is linear, the other is systemic as it considers complex relationships, feedback loops, and non-evident cause-effect relationships.

Where one requires commands from those in authority, the other requires leadership from those in authority (as I'll discuss in some detail below). Where one runs smoothly, the other is typically accompanied by conflict and distress. Where one demands precision and can be translated into protocols, the other demands creativity and gets restrained by protocols. Where one focuses on optimizing, the other focuses on experimenting. Where one calls for homogeneity, the other calls for diversity.

Realizing that today's dynamic reality requires far more adaptive work than ever before, it becomes easier to understand why it is increasingly important for companies to boost their employees' potential instead of limiting it. Technical work calls for using a specific competency or expertise that a person might have — sometimes one that is very complex and expensive — whereas adaptive work calls for using as much of people's capacity as possible, allowing for their initiative, creativity, collaboration, frankness, questioning, and mindfulness beyond their technical expertise.

There is no doubt that adaptive work is both challenging and attractive. But at the same time it is difficult and resisted. Difficult, because it goes against our natural tendency to look for equilibrium, and also because it requires a set of skills that employees are inadequately trained in. And it is resisted, because adaptation produces losses, or at least a sense of loss. There can be visible losses, like the loss of income, the loss of a title or job, or (when stress at work leads to stress in an employee's personal life) the breakup of a marriage. But there can also be invisible losses, like the loss of loyalties, expectations, status, power, values, self-confidence, and trust, to name a few. That is why it is so common for organizations to do technical work as a way of avoiding adaptive work. Sometimes this is done consciously, but most of the time it is done unconsciously. For example, technical work typically happens in mergers, where most of the attention is devoted to the financial aspects and little attention is paid to emotional and psychological issues; or in restructuring processes, where energy is devoted to the symptoms of the problem but not its deeper causes; or in internal communications campaigns, which are typically employed as a way of changing employees' attitudes and behaviors without doing the deep work that true adaptive change requires.

Of course, there are other ways of avoiding doing the necessary adaptive work that organizations are faced with. Many times executives and managers try to place the responsibility for their problems on outside forces, blaming political or regulatory authorities, bad economic conditions, unscrupulous competitors, social and local movements, or even non-responsive clients. Other times they prefer to overlook what is going on outside, thereby exacerbating the problems they have or will have. In other cases, business units, departments, or teams may blame one another. And in still other cases, organizations develop an oversimplified or overoptimistic view of the situation and simply deny that any adaptation is necessary.

Whatever the mechanism, the fact is that you should expect avoidance to take place as a way to minimize or get around the losses at stake. But the final result is the same: failure to adapt.

TENSION AND THE DYNAMICS OF CHANGE

The *Home Star*, HP, a government agency, an NGO, or any other kind of organization has a business or task to carry out in which all or most efforts are invested. Employees at the *Home Star* devote a lot of time to reporting the news and writing about it, to selling ads, to making logistics more efficient, and to building good relationships with the community. Executives at HP devote a lot of time and energies to developing new products, providing the best technological services, and finding more efficient ways to manufacture those products. It would be easy to provide a similar list of daily tasks for other kinds of organizations. It's normal and appropriate for organizational management to devote time and energy to these important tasks.

But how many top executives put explicit emphasis and dedicate time to developing their company's adaptive capacity? This is not a matter of doing something different from the daily business; rather, it is a matter of doing that same business with a broader perspective. In other words, while performing the tasks necessary to obtain the business or budgetary results, the interactions that underlie those tasks need to be made more functional, with a very specific goal in mind: increasing the organization's adaptive capacity.

Yet relatively few CEOs include a conscious effort to increase their organization's adaptive capacity as one of the tasks they undertake in their authority roles. And this is unfortunate, since the capacity to adapt is one of the most important ones for any organization today.

However, if CEOs are going to deliberately undertake the task of increasing their organizations' adaptive capacity, they'll need to understand exactly what this means and how it works.

What, then, are organizations with a larger adaptive capacity like? Based on the distinctions we have made, it is now possible to say that these organizations adapt — proactively or reactively — more easily to external and internal changes, effectively carrying out the adaptive work that is demanded by those challenges, because employees at all levels of these organizations have the readiness and abilities to face them instead of avoiding them.

This capacity makes a company more competitive in the long run by allowing it to create and take advantage of opportunities, to correct its course of action when needed, to be less dependent on the ideas and competencies of a brilliant CEO, and to deploy more of its people's potential.

The larger the adaptive capacity of an organization, the more and greater adaptive challenges it will be able to face, and will do so at a faster pace. HP, for example, ended up afterwards having a larger adaptive capacity than it had in 1999, when Fiorina started introducing the changes she envisioned. But this was the byproduct of a highly traumatic process rather than a well-thought-out strategy, and a big question mark remained in regard to the company's conscious and ongoing effort to keep increasing its adaptive capacity. You can learn to become a more cautious driver by experiencing a crash, as the increased adaptive capacity of HP today suggests. But taking the traumatic route may involve paying a higher personal price than needed — in this case, the dismissal of Fiorina from her post — and making that increase a one-step shock rather than a continuous and sustainable path.

It doesn't have to happen that way. You don't need to crash your car to become a more cautious driver; you can learn the same lesson in a less traumatic way if you set your mind on it. An organization can consciously learn to become more adaptive, working certain specific variables (discussed in Part Two). But this is something that needs to be on the CEO's agenda, the same way the business itself is on his or her agenda.

Jack Welch, as CEO of GE, was one of the first top executives to understand this. It happened after his initial years in that position, when he restructured the whole company (including making a number of controversial layoffs and divestitures) and earned the nickname of "Neutron Jack." But then what? Should Welch have continued to be on top of every executive, making every decision, putting intense pressure on every department to make things happen? That would have killed the company's development and would have also killed him. Welch understood, at that point, after dealing with the emergency of the early '80s, that his role had to change, and it did actually change.

In Welch's own words, "A company can boost productivity by restructuring, removing bureaucracy and downsizing, but it cannot sustain high productivity without cultural change."[10] This was his way of saying that a CEO — like Welch himself — ought to look inside the organization, analyzing and improving the way people interact among themselves and with others outside the company while doing their tasks. In the latter portion of his two-decade tenure as CEO, Jack Welch started talking extensively about the adaptive culture GE needed to develop, including the "boundaryless behavior" that every executive should embody, the continual development of leadership abilities, the 360-degree feedback process, the creation of an environment in which employees could be their best, and the development of anti-parochial attitudes. These kinds of initiatives and the priority that was given to them substantially increased GE's adaptive capacity, and it should be no surprise that this company is still considered the world's leader in executive development.

But building adaptive capacity is no easy matter. As we've seen, people resist change when they fear they might lose something. Roughly speaking, a person weighs losing something twice as much as he or she weighs gaining it.[11] This is why it is so common to hear "Now that I lost it, I realize how much I valued it." What's more, the losses are felt before the benefits arrive and, in comparison to the losses, the benefits typically appear more vague and uncertain. But eventually, when circumstances and the need for change are powerful enough, people do change, and so do organizations. And the more they are used to changing, the more adaptive they become.

Why is it that, despite the losses involved, a person or an organization may sometimes end up changing? As human beings, we change when we feel, for a long enough period of time, the tension that comes from being in disequilibrium, which in turn is created by a problem. In fact, everything starts from a problem. If there is no problem, people and organizations remain in equilibrium, in their own status quo. Why would they change? Only because they face a problem, which pushes them to experiment with new options, trying to reach a new equilibrium.

The problem, though, doesn't have to take the form of a crisis. An opportunity can also be seen as a problem — a benevolent problem, if you like. The essence of a problem is the gap that exists between our aspirations — as defined by ourselves — and the current reality — as perceived by ourselves. The larger the gap, the higher the disequilibrium, and the stronger the tension we feel. It's precisely that tension that makes us move and potentially change.

Adaptive change is, therefore, triggered by the tension we feel, but it only happens when we are able to remain in disequilibrium, holding the tension during that difficult period where the losses seem greater than the benefits and when the temptation of pulling back is strong.

Here's an example that illustrates how this process might work in a case of personal change. Jim was a successful operations manager in a company we will call Southern Energy. He was used to reaching the results demanded by company authorities at the corporate level, in response to which he received a good annual bonus and the appreciation of his boss. His professional life was in equilibrium, since he liked his job and performed according to the expectations that rested on him.

It's true that from time to time the human resources manager came to Jim with some complaints about his "authoritative and harsh management style," raised by certain members of his team, but since the good results supported his performance, Jim ignored them. In fact, Jim thought that his style was the key to that good performance.

Nothing was really generating tension in Jim and therefore he found no reason to change — until his equilibrium was threatened when a new boss was appointed. Sarah came from another subsidiary of the same corporation. After a couple of months she realized that the high turnover rate that existed among young and newly hired engineers in operations — a problem she had been warned about — was directly connected to the harsh style that Jim and two other older managers had embraced for years. A decade earlier, people were used to that kind of mistreatment and did not leave the company, but this had changed with the new generation and with the shortage of professionals in the industry.

Sarah gathered the evidence and had individual conversations with Jim and the other two managers, explaining to them that they had to change the way they managed their people. Sarah was asking the three managers to change — to engage in adaptive work. At first Jim found many explanations to justify himself, avoiding the adaptive work Sarah was confronting him with. But he started feeling increased tension when some other events occurred: he received negative feedback from his direct reports, he realized the corporation was engaged in a serious effort of introducing new organizational values that put people as the center of its mission, and one of his own children threatened to leave home.

Eventually, the tension was high enough to make Jim understand he had a problem. "Now I realize that I'll have to change my attitude and behaviors toward my people," he acknowledged to Sarah, accepting her offer of receiving the support of a coach.

During this period of adaptive work, Jim hesitated many times, going back and forth, trying to develop new abilities, resorting under pressure to his default settings, and being questioned by his buddies when he expressed his intention to do things differently. However, after a year of sustained adaptive work, people began to notice visible changes in Jim, which was not the case with the other two managers, who were eventually laid off.

It is not difficult to understand that facing this adaptive challenge was a hard test for Jim. He avoided it in the beginning, until the tension felt led him to question himself instead of denying everything and blaming others. He was able to keep up with this process of disequilibrium, finally reaching another equilibrium — a new and more sustainable one.

Notice a couple of lessons about adaptation that are implied in Jim's story. First, a degree of *responsiveness* to tension is crucial for adaptation to take place.

In Jim's case, this responsiveness was not very well developed. For example, Jim did not react to the observations of the human resources manager about his behavior with members of his team. Only when Sarah, his new boss, started saying the same things, forcing him to receive live feedback from his direct reports and then taking the opportunity to work with a coach — together with some events that took place at home — did Jim finally feel the tension needed to move him away from his equilibrium, little by little. Had Jim been more open to the initial signals about his attitudinal problem when exercising his authority, he would have assumed this adaptive challenge earlier and maybe more effectively, without risking the relationship with his new boss and some other top executives.

Of course, the two managers who were laid off showed themselves to be even less responsive than Jim. They never felt enough tension to face their adaptive challenge, despite the fact that both received the same feedback Jim did.

Being responsive to those signals that challenge the current equilibrium will allow you to feel more tension and react sooner to the problem you are facing, in this way eventually adapting.

Just as important as responsiveness is to the adaptation process is the concept of the *holding environment*, and this is the second lesson. Sarah created tension in Jim by showing him evidence of the effects of his behavior, by exposing him to feedback, and by showing him how the external conditions had changed and how the organization was changing. But at the same time she contained him, that is, held him, being explicit about how important he was to the company, offering him help, hearing him, and openly recognizing that this adaptive work would be difficult for him. Through these actions, she created a holding environment that made it possible for Jim to accept and cope with change.

As we saw, without experimenting with and internalizing the tension associated with his disequilibrium, Jim would not have changed; but without being contained within a holding environment, he would not have gotten into the adaptive work.

We see, then, that tension and holding environment go hand in hand. Tension is the source of adaptive work, but when tension is not contained it can be destructive. When there is disequilibrium, there also needs to be a powerful holding environment to make it productive.

THE EFFECTS OF RESPONSIVENESS AND HOLDING ENVIRONMENT ON ADAPTIVE CAPACITY

The same network of relationships among tension, responsiveness, and holding environment applies to organizations as well. Southern Energy started looking at the ways authority was being exercised because the larger corporation they belonged to became responsive to certain changes in the environment. Younger employees belonging to a new generation were more empowered and looking for a better balance between work and personal life, on the one hand, and the labor market was lacking professionals on the other. These trends impacted every energy company, but not every company had the same level of responsiveness, which affected their adaptive capacity. The sooner a company senses the tension created by new circumstances, the higher the likelihood of successfully facing the adaptive challenge posed by those circumstances. And an organization is in tension when there is a critical mass of people within it, including those who have enough power to drive change, feeling that tension themselves.

Having a greater responsiveness, therefore, is what allows an organization to respond to whatever change may represent a threat to the current equilibrium, letting the consequential tension be felt instead of disregarded or avoided. The change can come from outside the organization (linked to the labor market, the economy, politics, competitors, suppliers and the like), or from inside the organization (driven by new people in positions of authority, a different strategy or policies, alterations in employee's mood, rapid growth and the like).

Yet, having a greater responsiveness does not mean that the organization will undergo a wholesale adaptive process every time some tension is felt. It means that the organization will not avoid the signals and will take corrective action more proactively than reactively, running controlled experiments to adapt rather than reorganizing to come out of a crisis. The best way to test a person's or an organization's level of responsiveness is by counting the number of times either has been surprised by internal or external events. If the number is too high, they have been acting without responsiveness and therefore have been unable to anticipate those shocks. They embody the saying, "For the blind, every stroke is sudden."

At this point, we know that people and organizations undertake adaptive work and change because there is sustained tension, which starts with some sort of disequilibrium, created by a problem that is faced as a challenge. We also know that in order for that change to happen, the tension must be both felt and contained. If it is not felt, it will produce nothing but

(handwritten margin note: Reminds me of turbulence theory)

avoidance; if it is not contained, it can be destructive. Therefore, we can conclude that a stronger holding environment and a greater responsiveness build up a larger adaptive capacity. This is shown in Figure 1-1, where a stronger holding environment means raising the upper line and a greater responsiveness means bringing down the lower line, thus expanding the range of adaptive capacity.[12]

Figure 1-1. Disequilibrium and adaptive capacity

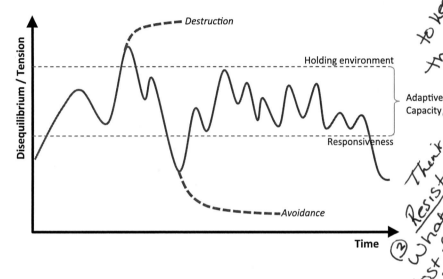

[handwritten margin notes: ① make people feel "safe"; Use authority to keep them in the holding zone; ② Think of Resistance as: What is being lost for this person?; ③ Expectation: Once you turn it back to them you will disappoint. Be ok w/ this. Paternal]

It is worth emphasizing that not every person or organization will react in the same way to a given level of tension. This means that a low level of tension may still generate adaptive work as opposed to avoidance, and that a high level of tension may still generate adaptive work, as opposed to destruction. This happens because there is a large adaptive capacity, which makes adaptive work easier because it allows the system to take advantage of a wider range of tension. On the contrary, when there is a limited adaptive capacity, chances are that avoidance will predominate or, in some cases, that the organization or a part of it — a team, for example — will break down or dissolve.

Increasing the adaptive capacity, as mentioned, requires strengthening the holding environment, enhancing the responsiveness, or both. You can attempt to run a marathon without being a regular runner, but you

[handwritten margin note: marathon metaphor]

have to be careful. If you try to do it with no training, you will probably be exhausted after a few miles, if not before, because your body does not have the physical and aerobic capacity to face the challenge. In other words, your biological system will not be able to contain the level of tension that comes from running. You first need to work to strengthen your own holding environment by expanding your physical and aerobic capacity through training consistently for six or eight months, eating healthy food, getting enough sleep, having a coach, and belonging to a team of runners.

But even that is not enough. What would happen if, during the actual marathon, the weather conditions were different than what you were used to or your body felt somehow weird? If you did not change your running rhythm or plan, you would not make it to the end. The fact is that besides having a strong holding environment, you also need a high level of responsiveness, one that will enable you to sense the tension as soon as circumstances change, mobilizing you to adapt.

Something similar happens with organizations. They can increase their adaptive capacity as long as their holding environment gets stronger, their responsiveness gets enhanced, or both. That may happen when an organization undergoes and overcomes a stressful situation — "What does not kill you makes you stronger" — as HP did. But it can also happen through a conscious organizational effort, as in the case of GE.

Strengthening the holding environment can be done in many ways: by pacing the adaptive work, infusing change with meaning, showing the benefits of the future, providing context, engaging people in conversations and new definitions, acknowledging losses, having change agents as allies, leveraging partial results, hearing employees' concerns, giving credit to the good things that have been done in the past, creating a sense of belonging, expressing affections, and building trust in the system.

Enhancing responsiveness can also be done in a number of ways: by protecting dissident voices, encouraging employees to pay attention and reflect about what is going on outside and inside the organization, making them feel responsible, discouraging defensive behavior, sharing information, allowing smart risk-taking, and exposing mistakes rather than hiding them.

The more these traits are present in an organization, the greater the impact of interventions aimed at generating tension and adaptive work. These interventions may include acknowledging that there is a problem, questioning the existing assumptions, naming the departments and people who will have to change, orchestrating the differences among factions, articulating feedback processes, hearing the external stakeholders — demanding clients, strong communities or engaged suppliers are key allies in generating progress when there is openness to listen to them — among others. In any case, because adaptive work takes time, the tension must be sustained for a long enough period of time, in different levels as needed, but always preventing tension's natural tendency to come down and end up in avoidance. Only when a new equilibrium is reached will tension no longer be necessary.

Once again, the distinction between technical and adaptive work becomes relevant. A technical challenge produces disequilibrium in the system because the organization cannot continue functioning as it once did. The solution calls for technical work, which means, as discussed, that the equilibrium will be rapidly restored and there is no need to sustain tension over time. For example, when a power outage takes place, generally there is know-how available and experts able to apply it to the problem.

An adaptive challenge also produces disequilibrium in the system, because the system can no longer function as it used to do. But because the solution calls for adaptive work, a new equilibrium must be reached through a process that sustains tension while requiring people to learn and develop new ways of thinking and behaving over time. This is what happened to Southern Energy, where some managers, including Jim, had to learn to exercise their authority in a different way. They had to live in disequilibrium for some time in order to adapt. They had to counteract the natural tendency to bring the tension down as a way of avoiding adaptive work and the losses that come with it, justifying themselves by saying, for example, "This is the way I am, and it has worked."

The same kind of challenge confronted David Franco, who eventually had to sustain a period of disequilibrium to effectively change his managerial style. Something similar occurred at HP, which, despite the traumatic tenure of Fiorina, was able to navigate those troubled waters.

THE U.S. MARINES AND THE ABILITY TO ADAPT

"Tarawa" was the name that Brigadier General Richard Natonski chose to designate the U.S. Marines' Second Expeditionary Brigade, which he was appointed to command upon its creation, less than three months before it went into action as part of Operation Iraqi Freedom in March 2003. One of four major combat organizations under the First Marine Expeditionary Force, this brigade was initially set up with personnel drawn from no fewer than ten different units, accounting for more than 7,000 Marines and sailors, with air, ground, and amphibious capabilities.

In the initial plan that was being developed for the invasion of Iraq, Task Force Tarawa would not enter the country until hostilities had begun, and would support another combat division of the First Marine Expeditionary Force, which in turn had the mission of distracting Iraqi forces from the coalition's main effort to get to Baghdad through the Third Infantry Division of the Army's V Corps. But by mid-February, when the entire task force had arrived at Kuwait Naval Base, the plans had already changed. Since all the coalition forces would now deploy from Kuwait, the eastern side of Nasiriyah — the fourth-most-populated city in Iraq — became a major strategic area, with bridges, highways, railroads, and waterways that needed to be secured to facilitate the movement of the forces heading toward Iraq's capital. That became Brigadier General Natonski's new mission. However, he no longer had direct control over the air combat and the operational support elements he had previously commanded, which reduced Tarawa's manpower to 5,800 troops.

On March 21, two days after a failed missile attack on one of Saddam Hussein's residences, where he was supposed to be meeting with top officials, Task Force Tarawa crossed the border together with the main coalition divisions, officially commencing the ground invasion of Iraq. During the first two days, operations evolved as planned, which allowed all the troops to move north, using the highways and encountering little resistance from Iraqi forces, which were rapidly seized.

But events changed dramatically on March 23, when Task Force Tarawa took the lead to accomplish its mission of securing all the crossing points in the surroundings of Nasiriyah. Even though the idea was to avoid urban fighting, 33 soldiers from the U.S. Army lost their way and got trapped in an enemy ambush; many were killed, wounded, or captured. Surprised by the news, Natonski was clear in ordering one of his colonels: "You have to do whatever you can to find those missing soldiers. They would do it for us, and we need to do it for them."[13]

That day ended with 18 Marines killed, in addition to the ambushed Army casualties. What's more, a friendly-fire incident involved two aircraft from the Air National Guard firing against U.S. Marines; the intelligence information proved to be wrong; the Iraqi forces' spirit was boosted; and the mission for the day was not accomplished. Even more important, the leaders of the coalition had begun to understand that this was going to be a different type of war from the one they expected. It was not going to be fought in the traditional way, with one army against the other, in a linear battlefield, weighing their military capabilities according to the rules of engagement established in international treaties. On the contrary, this would be a war fought in the cities against paramilitary forces that used guerilla tactics; blended with the civilian population; occupied hospitals, mosques, and schools as defensive positions; resorted to human shields, and had access to powerful artillery.

What was supposed to take only one day in the original plan was taking far longer. Meanwhile, analysts had already been drawing conclusions about the problems experienced by the U.S. military, despite its tremendous supe-riority, in fighting the Iraqi forces in an unfamiliar urban battleground.

But though Nasiriyah ended up being the hardest of the battles, it also became the best learning field. In the coming days, Task Force Tarawa changed some of its methods, and the tactics supplanted the bigger plans as headquarters recognized the need for on-the-field learning. They found that Cobra helicopters could be successful in halting rooftop shooting and destroying enemy armored vehicles; more aggressive patrolling was important in keeping civilians safe; entering residences could prevent enemy fighters from establishing safe havens; scout-sniper teams could be focused on gath-ering information that human exploitation teams could use in determining the location of enemy positions; and counter-battery radar and artillery could be utilized to neutralize enemy mortars.

Though the initial plan was to avoid entering the urban areas, enemy tactics and the initial successes of Task Force Tarawa convinced headquar-ters that the coalition could and should take control of the major cities. On March 27, General Natonski received the order to take Nasiriyah with support from other units, including Navy SEALs and Army Special Forces, which would report to him. On April 2, after eleven days of hard fighting, he was finally able to declare that Nasiriyah had been seized. After that, it took less than two weeks for the coalition to gain control over the country, announcing the end of major combat operations on April 14.

It would soon be clear that the conflict in Iraq was far from over. The successful conclusion of the ground war morphed into a long-term struggle for stability that would sorely test the adaptive capacity of the U.S. Marines as well as the military and political leadership of the entire coalition. But there's no question that the initial assault that toppled the regime of Saddam Hussein was one of the most successful military engagements of the post–World War II era, as well as a vivid illustration of adaptive capacity in practice.

Would Operation Iraqi Freedom have been successful if the invasion forces had stuck to their initial plan? In what ways did the concept of authority play a role in changing the plan and adapting to unexpected situations when needed? To answer these questions, let's first understand what's behind this idea of authority.

THE EFFECTS OF AUTHORITY ON ADAPTIVE CAPACITY

The authority role is and has always been an essential element of a group, no matter how small or large it may be.[14] And regardless of how that authority is appointed, an implicit or explicit social contract exists between the person who fills that role and the rest of the group, be it a family, a school, a company, a country, or the United Nations. That social contract grants the person in authority certain powers but at the same time establishes certain obligations that come in the form of services that ought to be provided to the group.

For several million years in the early development of humankind, authority figures were accustomed to attending to the needs of a group not larger than fifty people, whose expectations were rather simple and all connected to survival: find food to eat, be protected from external threats, and maintain order within the members of the band. Indeed, those expectations were typically matched by simply following the norms that had been inherited from previous generations. In other words, most of the work was technical and the role of authority was usually performed by culture. From time to time, adaptive challenges had to be faced, which created some distress in the group and required special attention from the authority. But the adaptive work was facilitated by the small size of the group, allowing the authority to know its members well and to build trust relationships that would provide a holding environment helpful in completing the adaptive work required.

This arrangement lasted until about ten thousand years ago, when the Agricultural Revolution started changing everything. As human settlements grew, establishing larger and larger social groups, authorities found themselves in the position of fulfilling the expectations of hundreds, thousands, or even millions of people. This was a major shift in society, and the whole concept of authority was subject to a big adaptive challenge. Similar adaptive challenges emerged again with the Industrial Revolution at the end of the eighteenth century and with the Knowledge Revolution some two hundred years later, both of which impacted the nature of authority so deeply that we are still trying to cope with the resulting changes. Nowadays, authorities are struggling not only with the number of people who look to authority in search of solutions but also with the increased complexity of satisfying those expectations, given the rate of change, the degree of connectivity, and the level of empowerment we are witnessing in a world where power is now distributed more widely than ever before.

In this new environment, exercising authority in the classical way — namely, taking charge, making the decisions, and giving instructions — doesn't work as it used to. As the problems we face become increasingly centered on issues of adaptation, they can no longer be solved by only a few who think and a great majority who execute. And because people are more empowered, they don't want to just follow instructions. Instead, they want to feel involved in the decision-making process. And this is true even when applied to warfare and armies.

As an expeditionary and first-to-fight force, the U.S. Marine Corps must deal with complex situations and uncertainty. Their air, ground, and amphibious capabilities provide them with the technical tools that are needed. But if they operated in the classical command-and-control mode, they would be too rigid and too slow, unable to take advantage of the judgment and initiative of their well-trained soldiers. This is why, despite being a strongly hierarchical organization (with ten ranks for officers and nine for enlisted personnel), the Marines are flexible enough to perform adaptive work when the situation demands it.

As the story of Task Force Tarawa illustrates, the Marines are well prepared to create temporary units with troops coming from different divisions, to listen to officers on the ground who can provide information and raise questions for the planning of next day's operations, to empower units to make fast decisions on the battlefield when necessary, to learn from mistakes right after they are committed and change as required, to experiment with new formulas if things are not working, to engage in frank debates and rapidly explore options before making relevant decisions when planning, and to collaborate with other armed forces.

Interestingly, junior officers in the Marine Corps no longer expect precise orders from their commanders but instead look for goals and general guidelines to fulfill them. Authority is very important, but so is independent judgment. And when the scenario changes, discussion takes place leading to fast decisions. This makes most people feel responsible and willing to take the lead when necessary, without resting on other people's shoulders, not even those of the high authorities. Without these traits, it would have been extremely difficult for Task Force Tarawa to succeed in the unpredictable, rapidly changing environment of Nasiriyah. The role the Marines assign to authority and the expectations they put on it favor the organization's adaptive capacity, making it possible to succeed where other armed forces would fail.

This was not the case with David Franco and his employees at the *Home Star*, however. The staff members at the newspaper expected the boss to make all the decisions, know all the details, take all the responsibility, solve all the problems, and mediate all the conflicts. His father had exercised authority in this way before him, and David had followed that same style for more than two decades. When he moved to another city to take control of the radio station and newspaper he had bought, his old employees didn't know what to do when faced with a dilemma or a situation that was new to them. David's hometown newspaper lacked the adaptive capacity to function without the boss.

By contrast, many of the employees in the newly acquired businesses were more used to taking the initiative, feeling themselves involved and responsible for the firm. They resented it when David took control over everything, limiting their participation, and many quit in disgust. These were two organizations with a larger adaptive capacity than the *Home Star*, but that capacity actually shrank under the leadership of an authority like David, who operated in a command-and-control style, creating dependency rather than responsibility.

One of the key elements of the reframed social contract in today's knowledge era is the idea of shared responsibility among authorities and people. Not every organization is there yet and there are profound differences among countries, generations, and cultures. We are in the midst of a transition, still experimenting with the disequilibrium that comes with it. Some organizations have made a lot of progress and are arriving to a new equilibrium, like the Marines; others are struggling with the tension and may be halfway there, like HP; and many haven't even started or are just beginning, like the *Home Star*.

In a broader perspective, if we were to compare the Latin culture with the Anglo-Saxon culture, we would realize how different they still are from each other in this respect. The former is more dependent on authority than the latter, which means that people in Latin American countries tend to blame authorities more easily when they are in trouble, avoiding their piece of responsibility.

This difference can be traced back to the independence process on the American continent, which differed in the British colonies and the Spanish colonies. When the British Parliament passed the Tea Act in 1773, the thirteen American colonies protested what they believed was a violation of the right to be taxed only by their own elected representatives, which ended up with a group of colonists throwing three shiploads of taxed tea into the waters of Boston Harbor. This was the symbolic beginning of the American Revolution, triggered by what was considered to be an abuse from the authority exercised over colonies with a higher sense of responsibility than dependency.

Almost four decades later, in 1810, the Spanish king was taken hostage by Napoleon's army when it invaded the Iberian Peninsula. But the Spanish colonies in America, instead of looking to themselves in search of their own path, chose initially to preserve the crown's power during the king's absence. In the highly centralized and dependent system they had lived in for three centuries, they were not used to taking responsibility into their own hands.

During the following decades the resulting vacuum of power was filled by charismatic authorities, or *caudillos*, in most of the Latin American countries.[15]

Thus creating a sense of shared responsibility, which is crucial to making organizations more adaptive in today's world, will present varying challenges depending, in part, on the larger culture surrounding our organizations. When facing adaptive work, it makes no sense to have authorities take all the responsibility on their shoulders, even if that is what people ask of them, because progress is only attained when people themselves change. And this will not happen if they avoid their share of responsibility by not being involved and by looking to the authority and then blaming it.

A key strategy that authorities should use in this effort of generating responsibility is *giving the work back to people*. This is a way of promoting their autonomy and responsibility within the framework of a common vision and a purpose, thereby increasing the organization's level of responsiveness and, therefore, its adaptive capacity. Authorities can give the work back in a number of ways: for example, by asking more questions and providing fewer answers, by holding steady instead of doing the work, by functioning through committees rather than giving instructions (though this can also degenerate into a technique of avoiding the work), or by fighting against avoidance mechanisms like blaming the market or the economy.

In the short run, authorities who follow this strategy of giving the work back may lose credibility, especially in organizations like the *Home Star*, because people expect them to take charge, not to give the work back. But in the medium- and longer-term, the organization will have generated more adaptive capacity, which will be the platform for sustainable progress that is not dependent on any person in particular. "If you want to go faster, go alone. If you want to go further, go together," as the African proverb says.

THE CHALLENGE OF EXERCISING LEADERSHIP

How large was HP's adaptive capacity? Was it enough to take on the deep changes Carly Fiorina wanted to carry out? In other words, how much leadership was expected from her?

Let's take a look at the mandate the board gave Fiorina when she was appointed as the company's main formal authority: "Totally re-create and reinvent HP according to the original HP Way." In other words, "We name you CEO and give you power, but you, in turn, have to save us from the problems we face and do so without producing much noise or causing us much discomfort."

Imagine being in Fiorina's shoes. How do you honor that mandate without frustrating at least some of the expectations embedded in it? Moreover, how do you make progress if you try to satisfy the expectations of more than 100,000 employees, not all of whom perceive reality in the same way or have the same interests and values? And beyond that, how do you satisfy those major expectations of change if you have ideas about what to do but no clear solutions?

Fiorina's major challenge can be thought of as making progress by disappointing some expectations and not being neutralized in the attempt. She did make some progress — but in the end, she was indeed neutralized. Why did this happen? Because HP's adaptive capacity was not large enough to resist the disequilibrium created by the adaptive challenge, and because Fiorina was not as strategic as she should have been when exercising leadership.

Authority and leadership are not the same and, in fact, people do not expect much leadership from their authorities. Instead, they ask merely that the authorities take charge of the problems they have by providing direction, protection, and order. By contrast, exercising leadership means confronting people with the problem, which makes people change, rather than taking the problem on your own shoulders, which does not.[16]

Authority alone is often sufficient for technical work. Providing direction, protection, and order will suffice where technical work is involved, because there is expertise that can be used and that only needs to be managed, allowing every person to do what he or she knows. People's assumptions, priorities, values or habits are not at stake, and therefore leadership is not required.

By contrast, when adaptive work needs to be performed, an authority that limits itself to giving orders, to managing, and to stating what needs to be done without exercising any leadership will fail in mobilizing people and obtaining results. Exercising leadership is an activity that one can choose to carry out or not, either with or without occupying a position of authority. But leadership is difficult to put into practice because it involves challenging people instead of satisfying them, asking questions instead of giving answers, generating disequilibrium and tension instead of providing comfort and safety, allowing differences to emerge instead of pretending that they do not exist, involving people instead of giving them instructions, and, in sum, confronting people with the problem instead of facing the problem by yourself or simply ignoring it. All of this must be done within a strong containing vessel, one that holds people together while they are living with the complexities and losses of adaptive work.

HP faced a big adaptive challenge when Carly Fiorina was appointed — in fact, that is why they appointed her instead of someone from within the company. But how much leadership did they expect from her? If asked the question, every single board member and executive would have said, "A lot." But in reality most of them expected a savior rather than a person who exercised leadership — someone who could take the challenge on her own shoulders and provide the solutions almost by herself, without annoying anyone. And she fell into the trap for a while, putting her efforts into brand building, inspirational speeches, media presence, and attempts to buy companies, all of which were more technical work than the required adaptive work and therefore aimed more for drama than for real effects.

This approach increased her credibility in the short run. But that did not suffice when she went for the deep changes HP needed to undertake. Because she hadn't built a strong coalition, because she had not prepared people for assuming the losses that would come, because she insisted on being the sole star in the firmament, because she did not pace the work, and because the company did not really sense the depth of the adaptation needed, she ended up being neutralized by those factions that were outraged by the changes she introduced and the losses the company was supposed to assume. Most of those changes were probably headed in the right direction, but to be correctly implemented and sustainable, they needed to be embraced by executives within HP, which is the adaptive work that Fiorina failed to do.

Fiorina needed to create tension within the organization, but since HP's adaptive capacity was small at that time, she should have consciously worked on strengthening the holding environment and enhancing the level of responsiveness. Here is where Fiorina failed to exercise leadership effectively. Given HP's limited adaptive capacity, she should have been more strategic, working on expanding that capacity before creating too much disequilibrium. Instead, she devoted a lot of time to the business itself, focused little attention on the organization, and didn't prepare people to face the problem and take responsibility for it. When she finally tried to do so, the disequilibrium exceeded the adaptive capacity, and she became the problem — and the scapegoat.

Short-term results are important to keep you alive, especially when things are messy. But thinking in the long term, those results should serve as an investment in support of the deeper goal authorities need to focus on, namely building adaptive capacity. This calls for strengthening the holding environment and enhancing the organization's responsiveness, which will allow tension to be productive. This will, in turn, allow authorities to make people responsible, thereby taking full advantage of people's potential, making it easier to exercise leadership to face whatever adaptive challenges come next.

And here is the paradox. Because of the depth and quantity of adaptive challenges we are facing in our societies and organizations today, leadership has become more necessary than ever before. Yet the role of authority has not evolved at the same pace as reality. This is why most of those who are in positions of authority get trapped, fail to exercise leadership, and end up performing ineffectively.

The dynamic is perverse: people ask authorities for solutions; authorities pretend they have them in order to gain and remain in power; they end up not delivering; people get annoyed, without seeing their own responsibility for the problem; and the authority is replaced, most likely by another authority who will not exercise effective leadership either.

This phenomenon is highly visible in politics, but it is also common in companies, especially in those that compete in dynamic industries or are undergoing internal adaptive processes. No one should be surprised to learn that the current "mortality rate" of CEOs in the Fortune 500 companies is higher than ever. Their average tenure is just 4.6 years.

All this only shows the difficulty authorities find in recognizing that their role has been changing, and that now they have to exercise more leadership than ever before. Authorities today must learn to mobilize their people to undertake the adaptive work that is necessary, instead of providing the fake answers that some people might actually prefer but do not generate progress.

The time for heroes, saviors, alpha males, and charismatic prophets seems to be coming to an end. Today that style of false leadership only generates distrust. The sooner authorities and people realize this and undertake the tough adaptive work that needs to be done, the sooner we will be able to mutually forge and live by the rules of a new, more effective and satisfying social contract.

CHAPTER 2

ORGANIZATIONS FACE PROBLEMS DIFFERENTLY

Everything starts from a problem — but not everyone faces the problem in the same way. Some people and organizations may simply avoid the problem, bypassing the challenge that comes with it.

Back in 1972, an Uruguayan rugby team, the Old Christians, flew to Chile to play a game against their peers in the Old Grangonians. Including the crew and some family members and friends, there were forty-five people on the charter flight across the Andes Mountains. The weather was bad on that Friday, October 13, and the aircraft crashed, immediately killing twelve of the passengers and leaving many more injured, three of whom died during the first night. The conditions were extreme, with temperatures that would go below minus 8 degrees Fahrenheit and scarce food reserves.

Those who were still alive had a problem and initially the way they faced it was by hoping for the best: a rescue. They rationed the little food they had, covered themselves with whatever clothes they had brought or could find, and took care of the injured. Ten days passed, and the group was still waiting to be saved when the team's captain heard on a little radio that rescue efforts had ceased because there had been no positive results.

Hopelessness took over the group. They were weakened, more had died in the previous days from injuries, and the rules the captain had installed to organize people now seemed useless. In this critical situation, two people took the initiative and faced the group with the challenge they had in front of them if they wanted to survive: "We are starving. Our bodies are languishing. If we don't consume proteins soon, we'll die, and the only protein we can find here is in our friends' bodies."[17]

The idea of eating human flesh divided the group. Many, of course, were horrified at the notion, which violates a basic taboo that most societies have obeyed for thousands of years. But some of the group recognized that this was the only way out, and accepted the necessity of it. Others refused the proposal initially but started giving in when they were starving. Others never ate and died. This was a personal and difficult decision to make. There were life histories and values at stake, there were religious concerns, and there were emotional loyalties to those who had taught them a way of being and behaving.

Different people face problems — and the corresponding adaptive challenges — differently. This is not just a matter of being more or less competent. It's deeper than that. It's a matter of assumptions, values, and beliefs, as well as attitudes and habits. It's not that we don't want to face the problem and change; it may just be that the adaptive challenge demands from us something we don't want to give away. That's why we resist adapting and why we get stuck.

This was the case with the Uruguayans: some of them adapted easily, some of them needed a mourning time to get used to the idea and bury their personal losses; and some of them could never adapt and died. In the end, after being isolated for 72 days, only sixteen survived, two of whom had the courage and strength to cross the Andes to reach help.

The same is true for organizations. The more easily and quickly they adapt, the better their chance of surviving and thriving. And, like people, different organizations face problems differently, because they have different levels of adaptive capacity.

LATAM AIRLINES AND SAAB: ADAPTIVE SUCCESS AND FAILURE IN A RAPIDLY CHANGING WORLD

It wasn't an impressive start to a business empire: a cargo airline with a single aircraft, two million dollars in annual sales, and an ugly balance sheet. The human resources behind the company weren't much better. The Cueto family, who bought the bankrupted company in 1983, had no experience in the transportation business and scant assets to invest; the oldest brother,

Enrique, who assumed the role of chief executive, was only twenty-four and had just graduated from business school.

Nonetheless, FastAir became the launching pad from which the Cueto family built what would become LATAM Airlines, one of the world's top airline companies, the largest in the Western Hemisphere and, during the second half of 2012, the world's leading airline in market capitalization. LATAM today boasts more than 300 aircraft, 55,000 employees, $15 billion in sales, and a multi-hub operation in South and North America, including 22 countries and 1,500 flights per day.

More impressive than the numbers, however, is the story of adaptation behind this success. It starts with the development of a global mindset in the heads of a team of young executives — many of them former classmates of the Cueto brothers — who were all born and raised in Chile, a country with a population of just 17 million located at the end of the earth, hemmed in by the Pacific Ocean and the highest peaks of the Andes Mountains. The only key player in the drama with a "natural" international perspective was Juan Cueto, patriarch of the family, who had been born in Spain and never lost contact with his homeland.

The development of global thinking proved to be critical in LATAM Airlines' fast growth, since it allowed the company's executives to understand that in an era of deregulation and globalization the airline industry demanded giant scale extending far beyond the frontiers of a tiny country at the edge of a distant continent.

Scale alone would not be enough, of course. An increasingly competitive airline industry also demanded high levels of efficiency, and an ever more connected world required great flexibility to cope with unpredictable economic cycles and uncontrollable events that could affect people's willingness to fly.

How to face these challenges? The decade that the Cuetos spent running FastAir proved to be the cornerstone of their later success, not only because of the experience the family gained in the cargo business but because of the team they were able to assemble, many of the members still in the company today. Having built that internal talent base, the Cuetos were prepared in 1994 to purchase and run a much larger company — LAN Chile, which had been founded in 1929 by the Chilean government and remained under its control for six decades.

At the time of the purchase, LAN Chile had 13 aircraft, 2,000 employees, $320 million in sales, and one hub located in Santiago de Chile. The Cuetos and their leadership team set about imposing the management style that had made them succeed at FastAir: dynamism, informality, speed, frankness, passion. Having taken a major first step toward becoming a regional player in the airline industry, they followed up with many smaller steps that would enable them to achieve scale. These included merging with Ladeco, another state-owned Chilean airline (1997); joining the One World Alliance (2000); acquiring local airlines in Peru (1999), Ecuador (2003), Argentina (2005), and Colombia (2010); strengthening the cargo business by opening terminals in Miami, Brazil, Peru, Ecuador, Mexico, Colombia, and Argentina; and setting up cargo alliances with Florida West (2000) and Lufthansa (2001). Finally, the biggest step of all, announced in 2010 and implemented in the following years: a merger with Brazilian TAM Airlines, giving rise to LATAM, under the control and management of the Cuetos, despite the fact that TAM was one-third larger than LAN in terms of revenues and employees.

Combining international scale with high levels of efficiency — which is critical in an industry that operates with low margins — without losing the distinctive advantage of quality service demanded real innovation. It came about through taking advantage of the synergies between the cargo and the passenger businesses, designing routes that would take both aspects into consideration and giving cargo as much importance as passengers in the business decisions. LATAM in fact came to be the number one airline in the world in terms of the proportion of revenues coming from cargo (one-third of the total). This dual revenue stream provided a unique advantage that enabled LATAM to operate with much higher profitability than most of their competitors in the airline industry.

LATAM also renewed its entire fleet of aircraft, designing features that could provide the best service to clients, the optimum division of space between cargo and passengers, and the highest degree of fuel efficiency. Decisions like these allowed LATAM to create its own low-cost model for national flights, following the trends of many other successful airlines, but without sacrificing service.

The airline industry has been hard hit during the past decade, starting with the Asian crisis in 1998, followed by the impact of 9/11, the rise of oil prices since 2007, and the subprime crisis in 2008, among other events, all of which put enormous pressure on airlines and tested their capacity to adapt. Many airlines have disappeared; others have suffered years of red ink. LATAM is one of the few to adapt successfully, having grown quickly during turbulent times.

Another industry filled with companies that have been struggling to adapt is the automobile business. This arena is the source of another exemplary company story — one with a very different trajectory from that of LATAM Airlines.

Saab Automobile originated as a producer of fighter planes during the Second World War. Faced by a declining market for military aircraft after the war, Saab created an automobile division as a way of diversifying its business, launching its first product, the Saab 92, in 1949. This was the beginning of what would become a sort of cult for a small segment of loyal drivers in Sweden, the United Kingdom, and the United States, who could be characterized as eccentric individualists, attracted by the innovative, unique, and quirky features of the Saab — aerodynamic design, a turbo-charged engine, sophisticated gadgetry, and overall robustness.

During its first three decades of existence, the company did fairly well. The Saab models 96, 99, and 900 were important breakthroughs that had a long production life, offering highly distinctive technological solutions. Saab's automotive division was never able to sell more than 140,000 units in a year, however, and its financial sustainability was always at risk. This fact was behind its merger with the Swedish commercial vehicle manufacturer Scania in 1969 and its partial sale to General Motors in 1989. GM took full control of Saab in 2000, only to sell the business in February 2010 to Victor Muller, owner of the small Dutch luxury sports automaker Spyker.

Muller was enthusiastic as he took command of the iconic Swedish brand. "We need to give our customers the clear message that Saabs will be Saabs again," he said. "The company has lost its DNA over the past years and that has caused its customers to turn its back on it. . . . We are not looking for new customers, we're just looking for getting our own customers back."[18]

Muller pushed hard to carry out this self-imposed mission. On October 28, 2011, he said, "I have had no life in the past two years. . . . My job was to save the company. I think I achieved it."[19] He had launched a new model that did not succeed, obtained financial support from Chinese car manufacturers and from the European Investment Bank, and made all sorts of attempts to find business partners. Muller's determination had scarcely flagged. Yet less than two months later, on December 19, Saab Automobile was declared bankrupt.

Was Saab condemned to disappear? Could it have adapted and survived? To answer this question, we need to understand the adaptive challenge it faced.

As noted, Saab enjoyed a modicum of success during the 1950s, '60s, and '70s. But things started changing in the automobile sector during the '80s, when Japanese cars became a serious threat to American and European producers, forcing deep transformations in the industry. Production costs had to go down and more efficient cars needed to be developed, which pushed all sorts of mergers, acquisitions, and alliances between companies in different countries and commercial segments in search of economies of scale. Another adaptive strategy that emerged during the early '90s was the use of shared platforms in the chassis for different car models, allowing for reduced development costs without compromising the uniqueness of each brand.

In this environment, it would be difficult for a small auto company to survive on its own. Not surprisingly, therefore, after reaching peak production of 134,000 units in 1987, Saab saw its sales decline in the following years, leading to a loss of $848 million in 1990. There was no way out but a merger with a big ally, which Saab found when GM bought 50 percent ownership for $600 million. This deal followed the trend already initiated with the acquisitions of Alfa Romeo by Fiat, Lamborghini by Chrysler, Lotus by GM, Aston Martin by Ford, and Rover by BMW. Later, in 1999, Volvo and Land Rover would be acquired by Ford.

It appeared as if Saab now had everything it needed to succeed: a strong brand, attractive technology, loyal customers, and the support of the largest automaker in the world. The challenge was to increase sales and reduce costs, which could be attained by maintaining Saab's identity while sharing a platform with other GM models. This is what Audi had accomplished: by sharing design platforms with other brands in the Volkswagen Group (including Seat, Skoda, and VW), it had boosted sales to over a million units while competing in the same commercial segment as BMW and Mercedes.

But Saab's effort to use the same strategy was not as successful. New Saab models were launched sharing platforms with Vectra and Opel cars from the

GM portfolio, but sales never really took off. At the core of this disappointing performance was a failure to clearly define and embody the Saab brand, caused by an underlying tension between the stubbornness of the members of the Saab team, who resisted giving up any aspect of the uniqueness of the cars they used to produce, and the unwillingness of GM people to understand and respect Saab's identity. Consequently, the joint leadership failed to engage in a dialogue that would allow agreement on what was essential and what was expendable in a Saab — a dialogue that would have been critical to their efforts to take advantage of the strength of the brand and come up with something that would have been more than a simple hybrid model with no distinctive aspects. Because there was no real interaction between the two teams, they ended up compromising, with each group adding part of the Saab's features, but with no real engagement for innovation. In the end, Saab fans would hesitate to buy the new models because they weren't different enough from a Vectra or an Opel except for the logo; and other potential new customers hesitated to buy a Saab because they weren't willing to pay the premium price.

For the twenty years that GM owned Saab, the division was a consistent money loser. When the global financial crisis hit in 2008, forcing GM into its own bankruptcy during the next year, Saab's fate was sealed. Sales had fallen to 20,000 units and, even worse, the car's identity had been lost. "Letting Saabs be Saabs again," as Victor Muller phrased it, was nothing but a dream at that point.

Other carmakers adapted more successfully than Saab to the challenges of the 1990s and 2000s, including GM itself. Another example is Volvo, like Saab a Swedish automaker with a strong brand identity and a small but loyal niche market. After being acquired by Ford, Volvo developed new models and broadened its niche, increasing sales. By the time Ford's troubles prompted Volvo's sale to Chinese manufacturer Geely Automobile, Volvo was well equipped to thrive through the next decade.

FOUR KINDS OF ORGANIZATIONS

LATAM Airlines and Saab Automobile tell us a lot about the nature of adaptation. They belong to different industries, but they were faced with similar challenges. Both Saab and LAN were small in comparison to their competitors, but each had a niche. Saab's niche was defined by the unique design of its cars, which was highly appreciated by the select market it catered to. LAN's niche was larger and fundamentally geographic, a holdover from the time when flyers used to prefer their own country's airline. Over time, however, neither niche was powerful enough to sustain its businesses — scale was becoming an issue. Both companies had a problem, and both tried to face it, but with very different outcomes.

In both cases, the strategy adopted by top executives was to join forces with competitors they could complement. In the case of Saab, however, the more adaptive aspects of that initiative — in particular, the need for collaboration and innovation among engineers from the two different companies — were never fully addressed. It wasn't enough to reach an agreement — a joint venture first and a full acquisition later — that focused purely on the technical aspect of the merger if the real adaptive challenge was not going to be properly faced. Here is where Saab proved to have a smaller adaptive capacity than competitors in the same commercial segment.

By contrast, LAN has proved to have a large enough adaptive capacity to remain alive and thriving. Its top executives knew that the industry was changing and that the company had to grow. Initially they started building alliances with some larger players, then they began buying smaller players in neighbor countries, and finally they took the big step of merging with TAM to become a global player.

However, this last stage has not been easy — indeed, it has seriously tested LATAM's adaptive capacity. The financial markets initially welcomed the merger; the stock price rose by 50 percent, making the company the world's largest airline in terms of market capitalization. But the expectations were too high considering the adaptive challenge that the conjunct operation created. Beyond the business strategy, merging structures and building a culture has taken much more time than anticipated, with higher degrees of complexity. Experience has shown that the two companies' realities are different, their processes are different, their systems are different, their languages are different, their mentalities are different, and their styles are different. Moreover, the merger has run parallel with demanding market conditions and fierce competition from Gol Airlines in Brazil. From its peak in 2012, the stock price fell by 50 percent a year later, and it's been slowly recovering ever since.

Will this merger be successful in the end? Given the high level of adaptive capacity LAN has shown through the last two decades in comparison to its competitors, answering yes would be a relatively safe bet.

Saab and LATAM are just two cases that exemplify the ideas that will be developed in this chapter. Because organizations are different, as people are, the goal is to help you understand what kind of organization you help to run, how adaptive your company ought to be, and how far it is from that point now. Later, I'll address the question of how to work through this gap as well as the specific variables that could be changed to make it possible.

We know that reality is more complex than a conceptual model. Yet at the same time we need to make some simplifications that allow us to understand that complexity and not get bogged down in it. The challenge therefore becomes to grasp the essence that is behind a complex reality without falling into reductionism.

Looking at the various industries that exist — and even at other sectors beyond the arena of for-profit private enterprise — we can draw upon basic distinctions already made and come up with two criteria that give us useful insights into organizational reality:

- *Technical vs. adaptive work.* The difference between one and the other lies in the idea of learning. When faced with technical work, people have to do what they already know, as opposed to adaptive work, when they have to challenge their assumptions, values, loyalties, attitudes, competencies or habits by learning something they do not already know. This also means that a command-and-control system of management is perfectly well suited for technical work but fails with adaptive work, when people's involvement is needed. Therefore, we can extrapolate and argue that more hierarchical organizations are required in industries where technical work predominates and that more participatory organizations are required in industries where adaptive work predominates.
- *Stable vs. unstable environments.* It is true that we are living in a world that grows continually more dynamic and uncertain. But it is also true that different industries and sectors face distinctive types of environments in this regard owing to variations in the level of competition,

the speed of introduction of new technologies, the pressures from external stakeholders, the degree of political instability faced, and the impact of natural forces. If these aspects are low, there will be little need to deal with this stable environment, people will look inward by default, and the organization will be more internally oriented. However, if these aspects are high, there will be a great need to deal with in this unstable environment; people will have to look outward, and the organization will be more externally oriented.

Let's apply these distinctions to an organization we've already discussed, the U.S. Marine Corps. It is pretty evident that the environment in which the Marines operate has become more unstable than it once was, considering that many armed conflicts now have less to do with national boundaries or areas of influence and more with identity issues. As a consequence, rather than nation-states battling other nation-states, we see nations or groups of nations battling amorphous non-state actors, like insurgent and terrorist groups, where new threats are constantly being incubated and the battlefield could be anywhere. More than ever then, the military, including the Marines, must be looking outward, at an environment that is full of active stakeholders, including the media, of course, and those allied forces with whom increasing collaboration is taking place.

Consequently, the nature of warfare has also changed. Instead of tanks, artillery, and airplanes fighting their opposite numbers, the primary means of battle have become ambushes, roadside explosives, kidnappings, assassinations, and suicide attacks — all carried out intentionally on camera for maximum informational effect. In fact, insurgents and terrorists are typically organized in cells, their motivated members using all kinds of technological devices that allow them fast and effective communication, making the cells flexible and unpredictable. From the military standpoint, this becomes a major challenge, because the type of work now required is becoming more adaptive, especially on the ground, which means that the command-and-control approach to leadership is becoming less effective.

For Task Force Tarawa, those eleven days in Nasiriyah were a vivid verification of this new reality. Initially, American intelligence failed to anticipate that Iraqi forces would concentrate on that city and also failed to understand the type of tactics that were going to be used, which reflects an inward-looking bias. (The same bias may help to explain the erroneous conclusions drawn by U.S. intelligence about the existence of chemical weapons in Iraq.) On the other hand, the ability the Marines exhibited in adapting to the unexpected situation they found in Nasiriyah reflects how prepared they were for performing adaptive work in difficult situations.

In the end, taking military control over the country would prove to be the easiest part of the broader goal of bringing freedom, peace, and stability to Iraq. The nine years to come would reveal how much more adaptive work that challenge demanded in comparison to the initial invasion, and how much more adaptive capacity is still needed in the military world, broadly speaking. Because its expeditionary and first-to-fight nature requires it to deal with uncertainty, the U.S. Marine Corps is one of the most adaptive armed forces in the world, and it should come as no surprise that it was called to serve in Iraq in the aftermath of the invasion even though its original mission had been completed.

The example of the Marines illustrates the distinction between more hierarchical and more participatory organizations as well as the distinction between more internally oriented and more externally oriented organizations.

A more hierarchical organization is one that has several layers, and a lot of weight is put on people who are granted formal power, leaving little space for questioning authorities or rules. A more participatory organization is one that has few layers and a lot of weight is put on people's ability to collaborate with others and make decisions jointly. In a participatory organization, authorities act as facilitators of the collaboration process, trying to assure that learning is realized.

A more internally oriented organization is one that will tend to put emphasis on norms, procedures, bonding, consensus building, and formalities, often trying to preserve as much of the status quo as possible. A more externally oriented organization is one that will put emphasis on clients, competitors, communities, social trends, and political events, always taking into consideration the messages heard from the outside and being inclined to challenge the status quo.

Of course, these distinctions have to be understood not in absolute terms, but rather as a series of variations between extremes. We saw this with the U.S. Marine Corps, which, like any other military force, is a hierarchical organization, but not as hierarchical as the Army or the Navy, and perhaps even less so than some government agencies or manufacturing companies.

When these characteristics are combined in a chart, as shown in Figure 2-1, we obtain four kinds of organizations, which we describe as *action-driven, bureaucratic, communal,* and *innovative.*[20] As we shall see, their approach to problems is very different.

Figure 2-1. Four kinds of organizations

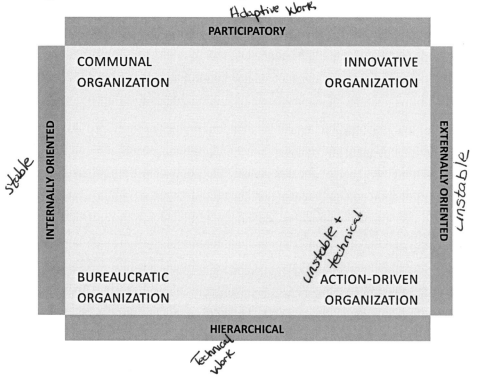

The four kinds of organizations named here must be thought of more as archetypes than as pure realities, which means that, in the real world, there will be companies that fall somewhere between a communal and an innovative organization, for example, or are transitioning between the two, or have divisions more clearly of one kind and others of another kind. The important thing is to define where an organization as a whole lies on this chart and where it should aim to be.

WHERE DOES YOUR ORGANIZATION BELONG?

The prescriptive aspect of our organizational mapping — that is to say, where an organization *should* be on the chart — is mainly dependent upon the industry to which the organization belongs. Specifically:

- If an organization is in an industry or sector in which the environment *Police* tends to be unstable and a larger proportion of the work is technical, it ought to be closer to an action-driven organization, one whose strength comes from understanding the trends that are modeling the industry and making decisions that get implemented as fast as possible. These organizations need to face problems rapidly because of the instability they live in, and without investing too much thought in them, because most of their work is technical.

- If an organization is in an industry or sector where the environment *Soc. Security office* tends to be stable and a larger proportion of the work is technical, it *Government* ought to be closer to a bureaucratic organization, whose strength comes from assuring that internal procedures and rules will be followed and applied without any discretion. These organizations are not used to facing problems because of the stability they live in and because most of their work is technical.

- If an organization is in an industry or sector where the environment *Microsoft* tends to be unstable and a larger proportion of the work is adaptive, *Google* it ought to be closer to an innovative organization, whose strength comes from having as many employees as possible looking outward and collaborating with one another to permanently challenge the status quo as they run experiments that put the organization ahead of events. These organizations need to face problems rapidly, because of the instability they live in, and thoughtfully, because most of their work is adaptive.

- If an organization is in an industry or sector where the environment *Schools* tends to be stable and a larger proportion of the work is adaptive, it ought to be closer to a communal organization, whose strength comes from members having a highly developed sense of ownership of the institution and well-established internal bonds. These organizations face problems very slowly because of the stability they live in, and they should invest a lot of thought in those problems, because most of their work is adaptive.

Figure 2-2 takes on the challenge of mapping representative industries and sectors within the parameters of the chart depicted in Figure 2-1. This exercise is based on my own academic knowledge and the experience I've gained teaching and working with top executives from a large number of companies and institutions in various parts of the world.

The first step in defining the gap that a particular company or institution faces in its quest to become more adaptive lies in finding the ideal location for an organization in its industry or sector as mapped in Figure 2-2. The second step is diagnosing the organization's current reality and mapping it into the same chart.

Figure 2-2. Representative industries on the chart of four kinds of organizations

If we think of a mining company, for example, a high proportion of its work is technical: extracting minerals and refining them in a process that is

well defined and that gets improved once in a while through the introduction of new technologies. Even the sales part of the mining industry is still highly technical, with prices that are established in the open market and buyers or brokers who are easily identifiable. On the other hand, a mining company operates in an environment that has become more unstable than it used to be, with high price volatility, an increasing shortage of qualified professionals, greater environmental and safety demands from communities, and more pressure from political authorities.

Taking all this into consideration, mining companies ought to be hierarchical and externally oriented, which means they should fall into the archetype of an action-driven organization, as shown in Figure 2-2. Yet like the Marines, mining companies will become more competitive if they gain more adaptive capacity; that is, if they move to the right and upward as needed. This might be necessary if the environment becomes more unstable, as with the boom of commodities in the late 2000s and the consequent growth of the industry, meaning that more adaptive work is required. Theoretically, it is tempting to get to the right middle point of Figure 2-2 or even higher, becoming an innovative organization, but this wouldn't be appropriate given the nature of the work that is performed by a mining company and the environment it is in, an environment that has nothing to do with the reality of, for example, an advertising agency or a consulting firm.

Are there any mining companies that are not action-driven organizations? Indeed there are, and they generally take the form of bureaucratic organizations, which means being one evolutionary step behind their rivals that moved toward being more externally oriented given the increasing instability of their environments. A good example of this is Codelco, the largest copper producer in the world, owned by the State of Chile, which has been struggling to develop more adaptive capacity, trying to leave behind the traits that characterize a bureaucratic organization.

WHAT IS YOUR ORGANIZATION'S REALITY?

Having mapped the industries in Figure 2-2, our second step is the descriptive one; that is, diagnosing the reality of a particular company and mapping it onto the chart to measure its distance from the industry's current state of the art.

There are, of course, many things that could be looked at when carrying out that diagnosis and determining how adaptive the company is. Part Two of this book goes into concrete variables that will take us down to the level of systems, processes, and practices, because they need to be examined if the gap is going to be addressed. But the big picture would be missed if we do not first understand the driving force and values that best characterize each kind of organization and thus provide us with an effective tool to diagnose a specific company. These are depicted in Figure 2-3.

Figure 2-3. Driving forces and values that characterize each kind of organization

[handwritten annotations: "Driving Force = why people act", "Adaptive Work", "Stable", "unstable", "Technical Work", "values — How people act"]

	PARTICIPATORY	
COMMUNAL ORGANIZATION		**INNOVATIVE ORGANIZATION**
SENSE OF BELONGING: Inclusion, Caring, Affiliation, Negotiation, Consensus		IMPACT: Anticipation, Creativity, Collaboration, Flexibility, Meaning
SAFETY: Formality, Process, Tradition, Regularity, Order		ACCOMPLISHMENT: Discipline, Control, Task, Efficiency, Results
BUREAUCRATIC ORGANIZATION		**ACTION-DRIVEN ORGANIZATION**
	HIERARCHICAL	

INTERNALLY ORIENTED ... *EXTERNALLY ORIENTED*

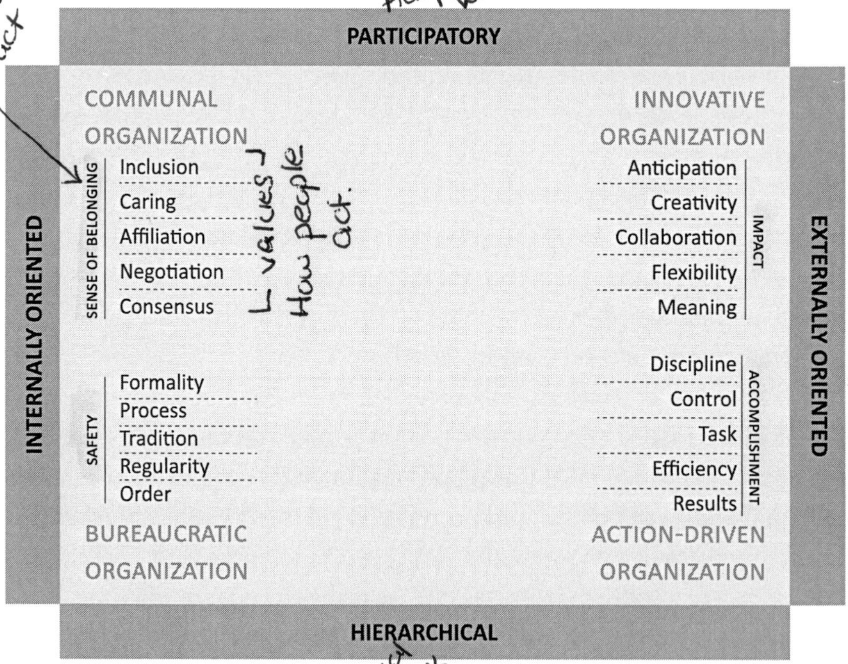

The driving force — for example, "Sense of Belonging" in a communal organization — has to do with what moves people into action. By contrast, the values — for example, Inclusion, Caring, Affiliation, Negotiation, and Consensus in a communal organization — have to do with the type of actions that should be expected. If the driving force defines the motive that explains *why* people act, the values define the behaviors that explain *how* people act.

In a communal organization, actions and reactions can be mainly explained by people feeling the need to belong to or be accepted by the larger group. This is *why* they act — their motive. When acting, they will typically look for consensus, affiliation, negotiation, inclusion and caring because they highly value these qualities given their motives. This is *how* they act — their behavior.

For an example, consider a church, which is the kind of social body that epitomizes the communal organization. Professing a faith in most cases is motivated more by being part of a community than by deeply believing in the existence of God. (Much the same happens with the boosters of a sports team or with a professional association.) And because this is the main driving force for people, these communal organizations will value behaviors that are aligned with consensus building and inclusion.

This is equally true for the other three kinds of organizations in respect to their own driving forces and values. If you examine the Chilean copper mining company Codelco, for instance, you will realize how the driving force and the values of a bureaucratic organization have been deeply ingrained in the company, making it very paternalistic indeed. And this should be no surprise: Codelco was created after the communist Chilean government headed by Salvador Allende finished the nationalization process of the copper industry in 1971. Before that, the large copper mines were in the hands of the most important multinational mining corporations, like Anaconda and Kenecott. As a state-owned company in a country where copper accounts for approximately half of the nation's exports — sometimes more and sometimes less, depending on the price — Codelco found itself increasingly trapped in the political system. Its executive president was appointed directly by Chile's president, and its board of directors was composed of members of the national cabinet and representatives of the workers. This created a complex network of loyalties, in which satisfying the expectations of each person's supporters was more important than improving the financial results of the corporation.

In a system like this one, therefore, it was almost impossible to lay off people, or even to run employee evaluations; executive positions were typically filled with political allies; and the executive president had little negotiation power with unions, because the government in order to avoid any kind of unrest preferred to cope with the high cost of the demanded benefits. Naturally, these conditions undermined the company's competitiveness, because important challenges were avoided, most notably the need to increase production capacity through the development of new projects with a different management culture.

In the end, Codelco's performance had less to do with adding value and more to do with fulfilling procedures, less with challenging the status quo and more with honoring traditions, less with creativity and more with regularity and order, less with personal accountability and more with collective avoidance, less with looking at the challenges of the future and more with resting on the glories of the past. In a bureaucratic company like the one Codelco had become, people's actions and reactions could be explained by their need for feeling safe, avoiding any kind of threat. That is why they would always stick to the process, doing exactly what was expected of them, but nothing else.

Could Codelco be a bureaucratic kind of organization and still be competitive? The answer is no. Things started changing in the industry when the price of copper dramatically rose with the commodities boom that began in 2005. New actors came into the game, production increased, explorations peaked, new technologies appeared, an enormous shortage of professionals was felt, and salaries increased. As a result, Codelco needed to change in various ways, but as a bureaucratic kind of organization its adaptive capacity was small, which meant that its production decreased and its costs went up more than the industry average. Talent began to flee as the company's competitiveness declined. Yet the forces inside Codelco continued to preserve the status quo, which provided the safety that most people in the system were looking for.

Eventually, the higher instability of the environment forced some people in the larger system to take risks and try to make Codelco more externally oriented and face the need for more adaptive work. The idea of changing the governance of the company began gaining popularity around 2006. Finally, in 2009, the law was changed to create a more professional and independent board of directors with well-defined responsibilities, starting with the appointment of the CEO. This was a turning point in increasing Codelco's adaptive capacity, slowly moving it from the bureaucratic kind of organization it had been toward the action-driven kind of organization it had to become, in which increasing numbers of Codelco workers would feel motivated by the willingness to accomplish goals. The types of behaviors that could be observed were little by little more in line with putting a higher value to planning and control, orientation to the task, discipline, and focus on results.

As expected, Codelco's movement upward and to the right in Figure 2-3 has taken time and effort. There has been resistance within the organization and many setbacks, including the departure of the CEO who initiated the internal change process in 2010 and resigned two years later. This is understandable, because the adaptive change required is not only about increasing the pace of decision making and moving faster but also about changing fundamental values, something that leads to important losses for too many employees.

Just think about what happens when a manager who has always been evaluated on his willingness to follow the process and make sure his people do the same is suddenly evaluated on his ability to increase the effectiveness of the plant he runs. In the previous scenario, he did not have to think very much, he had complete control over the situation, and he was taking no risk. In the new scenario, he will have to explore new ways to improve the operation of the plant, he will have to collaborate with other managers and departments, and he will have to experiment and bear the risks that experimentation always brings. Of course, he'll fear losing his reputation as a competent professional, the good relationship he has always had with his subordinates while acting as a protecting father, and potentially his own job.

When people used to apply to Codelco, their main motive was safety, namely, the desire to find a stable job. In 2010, more action-driven types started applying to Codelco, people whose main motive was the desire to accomplish something, in line with the change in values that was slowly taking place in the company.

When people apply to Google or Apple or Disney or 3M, their main motive is to be able to have an impact — to leave a mark on the world. They are looking for an environment that values creating new options, working with flexibility, collaborating with others who bring in diversity, anticipating trends, and doing something that is meaningful. These are people suited for working in an innovative organization, where unleashing everyone's potential is more important than following specific procedures or even attaining certain given results.

Thus, the perceived nature of an organization tends to attract people who will fit and strengthen the characteristics of the organization. This means that the nature of an organization tends to be self-reinforcing and therefore quite difficult to change.

Think about the driving force and values that mark your organization. Where does your organization fall on the chart shown in Figure 2-3? What type of people is it attracting? Are you satisfied with the outcomes?

EVOLVING TO BE MORE ADAPTIVE

So far, we have established four organizational archetypes based on two criteria: technical vs. adaptive work and stable vs. unstable environments. We have also mapped some representative industries based on those criteria. And we have indicated the driving force and the main values that best characterize each kind of organization. In practical terms, this has provided us with a way of understanding the gap that a particular company in a specific industry faces when it comes to increasing its adaptive capacity. Closing that gap is by itself an adaptive challenge the company has to face, which typically involves reframing certain values, besides intervening in a number of specific systems, processes, and practices, which are discussed in Part Two.

It should be clear at this point that not all companies and institutions are expected to be equally adaptive. That is why we don't talk about "adaptive organizations" as such, and why "the adaptive organization" is not considered in the chart as a kind of organization by itself. Rather, action-driven, bureaucratic, communal, and innovative organizations should all try to be more adaptive or to increase their adaptive capacities within the limits of their nature. This means moving upward and to the right in Figure 2-1, within those limits. For example, it is good for a government agency to become more adaptive, but always within the confines of a bureaucratic organization. If it moves too far to the right, the risk of arbitrariness becomes overly high, and if it moves too far upward, the risk of unaccountability is just around the corner.

Also, not all divisions and departments within a company need to be equally adaptive. Typically, for example, the sales department will have a larger adaptive capacity than the legal department. However, we can still talk about the adaptive capacity of the organization as a whole when comparing it to another company. No matter how large the adaptive capacity of the sales department of Codelco, it won't be even close to the adaptive capacity of the sales department of HP. And, of course, no matter how small the adaptive capacity of the legal department of HP is, it will be much larger than the adaptive capacity of the legal department of Codelco. In the end, regardless of the differences that exist among departments and divisions, each organization has its own character, and that is reflected in its overall adaptive capacity.

And I should also clarify that throughout this chapter I have been referring to mature companies when talking about different kinds of organizations, not to entrepreneurships or start-ups. Typically, these fledgling enterprises will have a larger adaptive capacity in that stage of development than afterward. This is why an organization will always have the challenge of figuring out "how to incorporate small-company attributes — nimbleness, speed, and customer responsiveness — with the advantages of size," in the words of Lou Gerstner, who led IBM's turnaround in the 1990s.[21]

In Chapter 1, I compared the need for companies to adapt to today's changing business environment with the need for living organisms to adapt in the Darwinian process of evolution. Given the fact that global trends show us that we are walking toward a reality that is every day more unstable and demands higher levels of adaptive work, all organizations — whether action-driven, bureaucratic, communal, or innovative — are permanently challenged to increase their adaptive capacity, which will enable them to face problems more rapidly and thoughtfully.[22] The more adaptive an organization is, the better suited it will be to face the specific adaptive challenges that its own situation confronts it with.

David Franco and the *Home Star* were ill prepared to confront the challenges created by the business expansion he undertook. Some of the initial survivors of the Uruguayan aircraft crash lacked the adaptive capacity to challenge their beliefs in order to confront the hard reality they faced. HP was too tied to its own past to confront the demands of an industry that had turned more competitive and more responsive to the customers' needs. And Saab Automobile was the prisoner of the icon it had produced and unable to challenge its own creation in ways that would allow the company to adapt to a new market reality.

The biggest challenge, therefore, is to make the organization evolve in a way that will always make it more adaptive. If this is properly done, the organization will have a higher adaptive capacity than that required by the adaptive challenges it will confront. Yet how do we know that the organization is less adaptive than it needs to be — that is, how can we tell whether a gap needs to be addressed?

Using the information in Figures 2-2 and 2-3, we can consider three possible comparisons, depending on the actual reality of each firm: first, between the company and the current state of its industry; second, between the company and the possible future state of its industry; and third, between the company and the current or future state of another industry it plans to enter.

If we are talking about a company that is falling behind in its industry, like Saab in the '80s, HP in the '90s, or Codelco in the '00s, it makes sense to start by making the first comparison and addressing that gap. If we are talking about a company that is organizationally prepared to move ahead of its competitors, like the U.S. Marines or LATAM Airlines today, it would make sense to make the second and third comparisons.

In making these comparisons, we may find that becoming more adaptive — that is, moving upward and to the right in the chart — may mean remaining the same kind of organization but with a higher adaptive capacity, or it may mean becoming a different kind of organization, more adaptive by nature. HP's challenge was increasing its adaptive capacity within the realm of an innovative organization. Codelco's challenge was increasing its adaptive capacity and therefore moving from a bureaucratic kind of organization to a more action-driven kind of organization, the category that companies in the mining industry have always occupied.

Increasing an organization's adaptive capacity is itself an adaptive challenge, which not only involves modifying systems, processes, practices, and competencies but also reframing values and facing contradictions among them as well as questioning assumptions when necessary. In most cases, however, top executives do not consciously examine this challenge; instead, they simply focus on the business decisions they must make and the tasks that must be performed. In other cases they realize that there is an organizational gap that needs to be addressed, but they treat it in a technical way, making changes in the organizational chart or sending their people to be trained in the skills they lack. Increasing an organization's adaptive capacity is both conscious and challenging work.

The first step in the process is understanding the underlying forces that shape a system, especially its values, as shown in Figure 2-3. Skipping this aspect would endanger any attempt to carry out a change in the organization, because it would mean ignoring the organization's identity and the losses that inevitably accompany change. Let's now consider those forces as they affect each kind of organization and the way it can be expected to evolve.

THE EVOLUTION OF AN ACTION-DRIVEN ORGANIZATION

An action-driven organization is suited to getting things done. People who work in it are primarily motivated by a high sense of accomplishment. In line with that, value is placed on disciplined behavior that helps in keeping the situation under control, and on performing tasks in a very efficient way, always with the attainment of results in mind.

These values of discipline, control, task, efficiency, and results constitute the essence of an action-driven organization, though they can be experienced on different levels or prioritized in different ways.

General Motors, LATAM Airlines, Avon (the cosmetics company), and McDonald's are all action-driven kinds of organizations, but since they operate in different industries, they assign a different weight to each of those values. The type of work that LATAM Airlines does, for example, is less technical than the work McDonald's has to perform, which means that the latter will be more hierarchical and therefore prioritize control more than the former. We can also observe that Avon's environment is less unstable in terms of competition and social pressures than what General Motors faces, which means that the latter will prioritize efficiency more than the former, being more externally oriented.

When an action-driven organization faces a gap between its current adaptive capacity and the required or desired one, some of the aforementioned values will have to evolve, which in itself is an adaptive challenge that will involve losses for people within the company. If we think of LATAM Airlines, as the company grew and became more complex and its work more adaptive, it had to start putting less weight on control and more on trust. Facing this contradiction in values was a painful process for many employees, who had to learn how to work with others in a collaborative mode rather than in a command-and-control mode. There was a loss of power involved, as well as loss of the certainty that comes along with control. In fact, many top executives thought that giving away control would lead to a loss of discipline. And since new competencies were required, more in line with interpersonal than task-oriented abilities, lots of managers felt incompetent for a while; a few never adapted and had to leave the company.

In a much milder process, but one that was still very adaptive given the company's obsession with control and standardization, McDonald's had to grant certain degrees of flexibility to its local operations and franchisees in the mid-'90s, allowing them to experiment with new ingredients in the hamburgers and in other products and practices. It was a tough decision to make, one that was resisted for decades but that was indispensable if the company wanted to gain adaptive capacity to thrive in a diverse world with more demanding consumers and varying dietary habits.

These are the type of losses that employees will typically have to bear when an action-driven organization strives to increase its adaptive capacity. These losses arise from the reshaping of some of the underlying values that are part of the organization's identity. Like it or not, this is a necessary part of the company's evolution, and often the most difficult one of all.

Another way to see this hearkens back to Figure 1-1 in Chapter 1. Increasing the adaptive capacity of an action-driven organization will demand strengthening its rather weak holding environment, which will move it upward in Figure 2-3 toward more participation. Its values are in line with a high degree of responsiveness, which is necessary when you want to be effective and obtain results in an unstable environment. But precisely because those values are so strong, there is little attention paid to people-oriented values like collaboration, meaning, and creativity. If an action-driven organization works on these values, it will strengthen the holding environment, as shown in Figure 2-4, and people will tend to remain at the company with a longer-term perspective, decreasing the turnover rate despite the higher levels of disequilibrium.

Figure 2-4. How strengthening the holding environment can enable an action-driven organization to tolerate higher levels of disequilibrium[23]

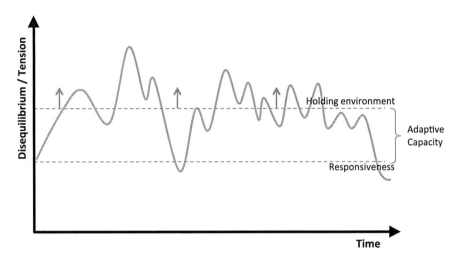

THE EVOLUTION OF A COMMUNAL ORGANIZATION

A communal organization is suited to seeking purposes that go beyond self-interest. People who work for this type of organization are mostly motivated by a sense of belonging, which is why the concept of community fits very well. In line with that, value is placed on expressing caring so that members feel included and on reinforcing affiliation through continual negotiation toward consensus building.

These values of inclusion, caring, affiliation, negotiation, and consensus constitute the essence of a communal organization, though they can be experienced in different levels or prioritized in different ways.

A local Jewish community center, a public school in Berlin, the Labour Party in the UK, and the community of writers and editors who create Wikipedia are all communal kinds of organizations, but since they operate in different fields they put different weight to each of those values. The type of work that a Jewish community center does, for example, is less adaptive than the work Wikipedia has to perform, which means that the latter will prioritize negotiation and consensus more than the former, being more participatory. We can also observe that the Labour Party operates in a less stable environment than a public school in Berlin, which means that the latter will prioritize caring more than the former, being more internally oriented.

When a communal organization faces a gap between its current adaptive capacity and the required or desired one, some of the aforementioned values need to evolve. Typically, a desire for a more effective and rapid decision-making process will exist within the community, but at the same time a high value is placed on consensus. This contradiction, which is based on the assumption that non-consensual decisions would generate a loss of affiliation, limits the adaptive capacity of the organization if it is not faced.

Traditional universities, for example, which used to be communal kind of organizations, have had to follow the difficult path that leads toward becoming more innovative organizations. Because their environment has become less stable, with increased competition and more knowledge being generated outside their domain, the pace of evolution has had to quicken and some members of the community have had to be left behind. As a result, traditional norms and practices, including even the institution of tenure, are increasingly being questioned.

Political parties do not need to become innovative kinds of organizations, but many have a low adaptive capacity when contrasted with the social changes that are now taking place. Party authorities need to put some critical issues on the table — purpose vs. power seeking, for example — which would certainly raise the heat, but they usually do not do that because they fear breaking the container that holds them together. Instead, they avoid the work by blaming the opposition or the government.

Even many religious organizations now face pressure to develop a higher adaptive capacity without losing their communal organization identity, which is a result of the growing changes that their constituencies have been experiencing over the last decades. The challenge is difficult for most religious groups, but perhaps especially so for the Roman Catholic Church, which resembles a bureaucratic more than a communal kind of organization, as we will see.

Referring back to Figure 1-1, increasing the adaptive capacity of a communal organization will require enhancing its rather low level of responsiveness, thereby moving it to the right in Figure 2-3 toward more external orientation. Communal organizations' values are in line with a strong holding environment, which is necessary when you want to keep people together. But precisely because those values are so strong, there is little attention paid to outcome-oriented values, like anticipation, creativity, and flexibility. If a communal organization works on these values, it will enhance its level of responsiveness, as shown in Figure 2-5, and people will tend to act and react more promptly, sensing and taking advantage of the disequilibrium before others do.

Figure 2-5. How enhancing organizational responsiveness can enable a communal organization to react more promptly to disequilibrium

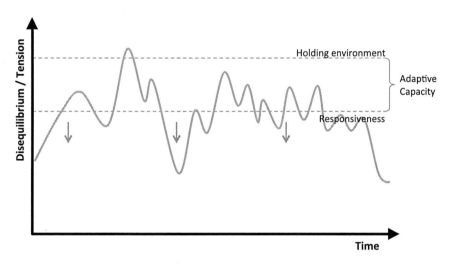

THE EVOLUTION OF A BUREAUCRATIC ORGANIZATION

A bureaucratic organization is suited to fulfilling norms. People who work in it are mostly motivated by a need for safety, which makes them avoid any sort of risk, often resulting in a highly paternalistic culture. In line with that, value is placed on the consistency derived from following the formalities that are associated with regularity, well-established processes, and respecting the traditions that come from a clear and long-standing institutional order.

These values of formality, process, tradition, regularity, and order constitute the essence of a bureaucratic organization, though they can be experienced on different levels or prioritized in different ways.

In most countries, the judiciary, the public transportation system, and the local electricity utility are all bureaucratic kinds of organizations, as the United Nations is, but because they operate in different industries they assign different weight to each of those values. The type of work that a public transportation system does, for example, is less technical than the work an electricity company has to perform, which means that the latter will prioritize formality more than the former, being more hierarchical. We can also observe that the United Nations operates in a less stable environment than a national judiciary does — in fact, in the European system, judges are supposed to ignore the environment, focusing only on the law and the case being judged. This means that the judiciary will prioritize regularity more than the UN, being more internally oriented.

When a bureaucratic organization faces a gap between its current adaptive capacity and the required or desired one, some of the aforementioned values will have to evolve. Typically, traditions and regularity are paramount in these situations, taking precedence over values more connected to creativity, results, or even negotiation. Though we are used to seeing bureaucratic organizations in the public sector as well as in the regulated part of the private sector, especially among monopolies, there are also many bureaucratic companies in the private manufacturing industry. Many of these have huge gaps to close if they hope to survive.

At Saab Automobile, for example, the excess weight given to tradition and processes made it too difficult for the company to overcome the losses that most of its people had to bear in order to regain competitiveness. The gap with the rest of the industry, which was more in the action-driven kind of organization space, was too great, making survival impossible when the environment became unstable during the global financial crisis in 2008.

By contrast, many public sector organizations, despite their adaptive challenges, should remain bureaucratic kinds of organizations, since most of the values they hold are connected to the reason why they exist. For example, though the Internal Revenue Service might benefit from reducing its loyalty to tradition in a quest for greater efficiency, we definitely wouldn't want it to start skipping processes or becoming less formal.

Some bureaucratic organizations actually assign value to some processes that have no meaning at all, except for the value that tradition in itself may hold. The Catholic Church is a good example of a bureaucratic kind of organization dealing with this adaptive challenge. Its current chief officer, Pope

Francis, has put this issue at the center of his own mandate, connecting to Jesus' own assertions that the norm itself must never be given greater value than its underlying purpose; for example, in his statement, "The Sabbath was made for man, not man for the Sabbath." Yet the Church, like many institutions in the public sector, bases some of the justification for its very existence on the application of procedures whose purpose and meaning are no longer obvious.

Referring back to Figure 1-1, increasing the adaptive capacity of a bureaucratic organization will require strengthening its weak holding environment and, especially, enhancing its low level of responsiveness, which will move it upward and to the right in Figure 2-3 toward more participation and, especially, more external orientation. Its values are in line with conservation, not with change, which functions well when technical work is demanded and the environment is stable. If the work becomes less technical or the environment becomes less stable, more attention will have to be directed toward people-oriented values like collaboration, meaning, and diversity, or on outcome-oriented values like anticipation, efficiency, and results. If a bureaucratic organization works on these values, it will strengthen the holding environment and will enhance the level of responsiveness, as shown in Figure 2-6, and people will tend to act and react more promptly, remaining in the organization despite the higher levels of disequilibrium.

Figure 2-6. How strengthening the holding environment and enhancing organizational responsiveness can enable a bureaucratic organization to tolerate and react more promptly to higher levels of disequilibrium

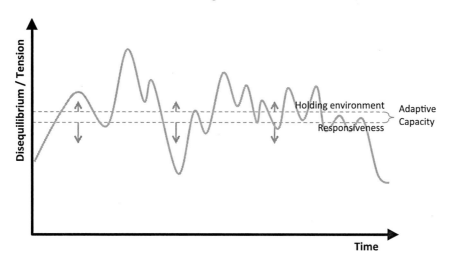

THE EVOLUTION OF AN INNOVATIVE ORGANIZATION

An innovative organization is suited to challenging the state of the art. People who work in it are mostly moved by the need to produce impact, which is why they will try to make a difference or leave a mark. In line with that, value is placed on doing meaningful work, which requires anticipation and creativity in reaching those places that others have not yet reached. At the same time, collaboration and flexibility are paramount in boosting the group's potential to imagine those places, letting everyone deploy his and her capabilities to the fullest.

These values of anticipation, creativity, collaboration, flexibility, and meaning constitute the essence of an innovative organization, though they can be experienced at different levels or prioritized in different ways.

Google, CNN, Amazon, and McKinsey & Company (the world's most prestigious consulting firm) are all innovative kinds of organizations, but since they operate in different fields they assign different weight to each of those values. The type of work that Amazon does, for example, is less adaptive than the work Google has to perform, which means that the latter will prioritize flexibility more than the former, being more participatory. We can also observe that McKinsey's environment is less unstable in terms of unexpected events occurring than CNN's environment, which means that the latter will prioritize anticipation more than the former, being more externally oriented.

Innovative organizations are the most adaptive, but they still may face gaps between their current adaptive capacity and the required or desired capacity, meaning that some of the aforementioned values will have to evolve. Thinking about Microsoft, for example, it is pretty clear that the recipe for its past success has not been enough for it to keep up with its rivals in today's high-tech arena. Relying on the intellectual property generated by software development, the company's largest source of income, is a dubious strategy in a world where the whole idea of intellectual property is being challenged and where free open-source programs are taking over. Microsoft knows this, but, despite its best efforts, it has had difficulty moving its people into new terrains to compete with companies like Google, Apple, and Facebook. Going into the unknown certainly generates the fear of lacking the competencies needed for success, which is why people pull back, even unconsciously, and want to continue doing what they know.

Yet even Apple faces a gap in its adaptive capacity, connected to its founder's death in 2011. Much of the company's success was based on Steve

Jobs' creativity in developing new products and his obsession in pushing the boundaries of perfection. Anticipation and meaning ranked very high in the company's value system, but collaboration and flexibility were not highlighted enough while Jobs was still alive. Now that he is gone, Apple's people have to learn to practice collaboration among themselves, providing higher degrees of flexibility for experimentation and mistakes.

Referring back to Figure 1-1, the adaptive capacity of an innovative organization is already large, with a strong holding environment and a high level of responsiveness, positioning it close to the upper right-hand corner in Figure 2-3, with high levels of participation and external orientation. Its values are more in line with change than conservation, which enable it to function well in light of the adaptive work and unstable environment in which an innovative company typically performs. Nevertheless, there will be always the space — and often the need — to become even more adaptive, which may demand paying more attention to people-oriented values, such as collaboration, meaning, and diversity, or to outcome-oriented values, such as anticipation, creativity, and flexibility. If an innovative organization deepens these values, it will continue strengthening the holding environment and enhancing the level of responsiveness, as shown in Figure 2-7, and people will tend to act and react more promptly, remaining in the organization despite the higher levels of disequilibrium.

Figure 2-7. How strengthening the holding environment and enhancing organizational responsiveness can enable an innovative organization to tolerate and react more promptly to higher levels of disequilibrium

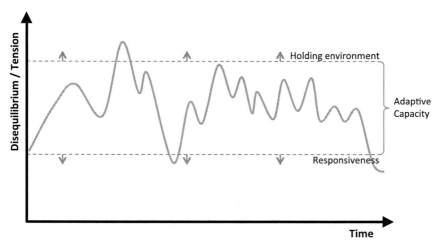

Based on the distinctions laid out in Chapter 1, in this second chapter we have developed a model that distinguishes among four kinds of organizations: action-driven, bureaucratic, communal, and innovative, with the values that characterize each. Most organizations are not pure examples of any one of these archetypes, but rather share traits of some of them, allowing us to map each organization in a chart that locates their adaptive capacities in comparison to those of other companies.

This is important, because not all organizations are called to be equally adaptive, though all are called to increase their adaptive capacity within the limits of their nature, trying to be ahead of their competitors.

As you seek to increase your organization's adaptive capacity, reshaping or even challenging certain values may be necessary, allowing the organization to transition from some of its more traditional ways of doing things to new ways. Because this is not easy to carry out, in the next chapter we'll examine how this evolution takes place in practice, emphasizing the need for defining the adaptive challenge and designing a process.

CHAPTER 3

THE PROBLEM AS AN ADAPTIVE CHALLENGE

Summary

We've said that everything starts from a problem. We've also said that organizations — and people — face problems differently, depending on how large their adaptive capacity is. The larger the adaptive capacity, the more rapidly and thoughtfully an organization (or an individual) will face problems, taking them as challenges that ought to mobilize people to do adaptive work. And the more adaptive work the organization performs, the more its adaptive capacity will increase. It's a virtuous cycle.

When Lou Gerstner took over IBM in April 1993 as the first CEO from outside the company, things were not looking good for the company. In fact, 1991 had been IBM's first year in the red since its creation in 1911, and the company's market capitalization had dropped by almost three-fourths in the previous six years.

Mainframes had been IBM's core business during the past decades. However, in the early 1980s, personal computers started displacing mainframes, and IBM became a key player in this new market. In the process, it forfeited what had been one of its key competitive advantages: integrated solutions made in-house. Instead of developing its own microprocessors and software, IBM bought them from Intel and Microsoft, respectively, which opened the gate for new competitors to manufacture personal computers, such as Compaq and Dell, and for other players in new commercial lines in the information technology business to make printers, disk drives, and database software in addition to processors and desktop software. Competition, therefore, became increasingly intense, which made it more difficult for Big Blue to keep pace and add value.

In 1985, John Fellows Akers, who had entered the company in 1960, was appointed as the new CEO (adding the title of chairman in 1986), but things didn't go any better. On the contrary, IBM's position in the market fell year after year, until it suffered its first year of losses in 1991. One year later, the company reported the biggest loss in the history of corporate America: eight billion dollars. This extreme situation forced the Board of Directors to make the decision to replace Akers with an outsider. Potential successors included Apple's John Sculley, Motorola's Chairman George Fisher, and even Bill Gates of Microsoft, but all three reportedly turned down the position.

Lou Gerstner didn't know much about the technology business: he had been CEO of RJR Nabisco, a food and tobacco company, and of American Express Travel. But it took him only a few months to recognize IBM's adaptive challenge. It had nothing to do with the quality of the computers produced and everything to do with the way people were working. Instead of looking outward, they were looking inward, and instead of finding ways to collaborate among divisions and departments to be more innovative, they were finding ways to reinforce the silos or territorial behavior that divided them.

When Gerstner assumed power, there was a plan to split IBM into the so-called Baby Blues, a collection of autonomous business units that could compete more effectively in each of the now segmented markets they operated in. This disintegration would supposedly make each of these spinoffs more nimble and less costly. Based on his assessment, however, Gerstner halted the plan and announced his intention to lead IBM in the exact opposite direction: greater integration.

In Gerstner's view, IBM's greatest and enduring strength was its ability to provide integrated solutions for customers, an advantage that would be lost if the company followed the breakup path. At the same time, it was obvious that the way IBM people were working didn't take full advantage of this ability, not only because they didn't add value when producing commodities like personal computers but because they were neither focusing on customers nor collaborating to serve them.

The fact that IBM had a problem was undeniable. Lou Gerstner reframed it as a challenge he called "One IBM." The company had to shift from being a hardware producer to being a solutions provider, a shift that could only be attained if people worked in an integrated mode, understanding customers and collaborating to put all their knowledge and competencies at their service regardless of the division they were in. And Gerstner knew that deeply ingrained values in IBM had to change for that to happen. As he put it years later, "I came to see, in my decade at IBM, that culture is not just one aspect of the game. It is the game."[24]

Powerful Statement

But Gerstner also knew that for change to be sustainable reframing the values that shape the culture would not be enough. Collaboration, entrepreneurship, a focus on customer satisfaction, and a sense of urgency needed to be expressed in concrete organizational variables, connected to systems, processes, practices, and competencies. To make this happen required modifying the compensation structure, the rules for getting promotions, the product development process, and the dynamic of the corporation's business review meetings, among many other things.

As Gerstner quickly realized, sustainable improvements in performance in an increasingly dynamic world have less to do with making specific business decisions and more with augmenting the organization's adaptive capacity. This meant closing the gap that he identified, starting by reshaping the company's values and then making a series of concrete changes in specific systems, processes, practices, and competencies. The changes he instituted have allowed IBM to regain its position as one of the world's leading companies.

The kind of change that Gerstner carried out in his successful decade at IBM is what top executives do when they have developed a level of consciousness that allows them to see the link between competitiveness and adaptive capacity, and when they have the willingness and courage to address this challenge.

TELEFONICA AND THE PROCESS OF ADAPTATION

It was unusual to see Matthew Key wearing a tie, unlike all of his colleagues in Telefonica's executive committee, who dressed in formal suits. In fact, he was the youngest member of the company's top team and its only non-Spanish native speaker. He didn't have a computer, not even a laptop, only an iPad, which he took in his frequent travels around the world from his office in London.

In September 2011, as part of a reorganization aimed at actively participating in the digital world and gaining synergies for international growth, Key was appointed the top executive of the newly created Telefonica Digital, one of the four divisions that made up the Spanish company. The others included the also new Global Resources division, headed by Argentinean Guillermo Ansaldo, the other non-Spanish member of the Executive Committee, and the preexisting European and Latin American divisions.

Telefonica was one of the top five telecommunications companies in the world, with a presence in Europe, Latin America, and Asia; it operated in twenty-four countries and had over 300 million customers. It had also been one of the few European companies to be listed in the Dow Jones Global Titans Index, which includes the 50 largest companies in the world.

Compañía Telefónica Nacional de España (Telefonica's original name) was founded in 1924 as a private company that was granted the monopoly of telephone services by the Spanish government. It was nationalized in 1945 when the state took control of it, though keeping some of the private owners as its partners, most notably International Telephone and Telegraph (ITT). Despite some privatization initiatives and stock sales during the '80s and '90s under the Socialist Party (PSOE) regime, the company remained under state control until 1997, when the conservative Popular Party Government sold all the remaining shares that were still owned by the state. That happened in parallel with the deregulation of the telecommunications industry in Spain, which meant that in 1998, for the first time in its history, Telefonica was a private company competing in an open market.

In preparation for this step, the recently elected government had in 1996 appointed a new chairman of the company. Juan Villalonga was an energetic forty-three-year-old professional who had held executive positions in financial and consulting firms, and had helped conservative politicians in defining the broad privatization strategy, but had no experience in telecommunications. He replaced Cándido Velázquez-Gaztelu, who was sixty years old and had been the chairman for eight years, after having spent most of his professional life in Tabacalera, the state-owned tobacco company, which he ended up heading.

It did not take long for Villalonga to start making profound changes, exhibiting a very different style from his predecessors, even though initially the company was still controlled by the state and had virtually no competition. In a nod to his financial background, he aggressively moved Telefonica toward making acquisitions and launching initiatives that would enhance its market value. One of the most remarkable was the purchase of several Internet companies in Spain and Latin America, which together gave rise to Terra Networks, a subsidiary that became the largest European Internet firm in market capitalization. He continued with the acquisitions of the largest telecommunication companies in the countries of Latin America, entering Brazil, among others, and transforming Telefonica into the main operator in the region. He even went beyond the telecommunications industry, acquiring newspapers as well as television and radio networks.

Villalonga reorganized the company by product lines instead of regional divisions, making evident that Telefonica had become an integrated telecommunications operator rather than the telephone services provider that it once was. Between 1996 and 2000, the market value of the company rose by a factor of four, suggesting how successful the organization was in adapting to the new reality of a deregulated industry that brought new competitors to Spain, its most important market at that time.[25]

In 2000, Villalonga was forced to step down after being accused of misusing privileged information, charges of which he was ultimately absolved. He was replaced by César Alierta, a fifty-five-year-old executive with a strong financial background, who had recently carried out Tabacalera's privatization and had served on Telefonica's Board of Directors for the last three years. He was more reserved and less decision-driven than his predecessor, which initially made him the target of critics who considered the company stagnant, and its only visible initiatives those previously promoted by Villalonga, including expansion into Mexico and new licenses to operate in Europe.

It's true that Alierta during the first two years emphasized cost and management controls, consideration of the broader economic situation, and improvement of the company's relationships with regulators. But starting in 2003, Telefonica regained momentum, strengthening its presence in Latin America, acquiring important assets in the United Kingdom, Germany, and Ireland, building alliances in Italy and China, and obtaining mobile licenses in more countries. The number of clients increased fourfold in ten years. To make this rapid growth sustainable, Alierta became increasingly conscious of the importance of human capital, considering it among the three key factors that explained the company's success: "Telefonica has an accumulation of talent unlike any I've seen either before or after coming here. Managing brilliant people is not easy, but their talent allows you to attain goals that are otherwise impossible."[26]

By 2011, Telefonica had become a multinational company, providing all types of telecommunication services: fixed and mobile telephony, Internet and data, paid television, web contents, and contact centers. But Alierta realized that this was not enough to serve the level of hyper-connectivity toward which societies were migrating. Furthermore, Telefonica's internal processes did not reflect the new world that was surfacing. More transversality, flexibility, global thinking, innovation, and agility were demanded.

The company's structure and culture both needed to change. The new divisions of Telefonica Digital and Global Resources addressed the former need; the arrival of Matthew Key addressed the latter. Key recognized that crucial new businesses in such areas as venture capital, eHealth, cloud computing, mobile advertising, and machine-to-machine services could not be successfully carried out under Telefonica's traditional vertically siloed organization. He also recognized that his most important challenge was to take full advantage of the talent potential within the company. This is why he assembled a team of 2,500 professionals from different divisions to build the London-based Telefonica Digital, whose mission would be to lead the process of strategic innovation for the entire corporation.

LESSONS FROM HISTORY: PEOPLE ARE ESSENTIAL

IBM and Telefonica have managed to survive for a century, from the early times of the industrial era until today's knowledge era. In fact, they embody the changes that the world has gone through during this period. The transition from one era to the next has been painful, but for these two companies it has also been successful.

Most companies, however, can't make the same claim. In 1917, *Forbes* magazine created its first list of the 100 largest American companies. Today, only nine of the original 100 remain in the equivalent list that *Fortune* publishes each year, and fewer than 20 have even survived.[27] One of the companies that was not in the first list, but is now — and has been there for decades — is IBM, which, according to *Forbes*, is also one of the 50 largest world companies, along with Telefonica.[28]

If we take a look at the S&P 500 — the index of the 500 most valuable companies in the United States — the story looks even more dramatic. In 1958, the average longevity of those firms was 61 years. It fell to 25 years in 1980 and reached 18 years two decades later. Moreover, in the last decade, half of those companies have been replaced. Among the newcomers we can count Google, Amazon, and Netflix, while those that have departed include Kodak, the *New York Times*, Palm, and HP. Notably, the only firm that has remained in the index since its creation in 1926 is General Electric.[29]

Regardless of their nature, organizations are living under unprecedented pressure to face adaptive change. This is not an entirely new phenomenon, but it has accelerated enormously during the last decades and is likely to keep accelerating in the decades to come. In explaining this, we could talk about trends related to technological development, increasing levels of education and wealth, environmental and social concerns, women and new generations coming into the workforce, a flatter and more urban world, and many others. But instead of talking about the future, let's try to understand the present by looking at the past.

Our ancestors have inhabited Earth for several million years. Yet, very little has changed in their way of life until only ten thousand years ago, when agriculture was invented. Before that, the various species of humans survived as hunters and gatherers, moving in small groups from one place to another, chasing animals and looking for more fertile zones in which to collect naturally growing foodstuffs. But when environmental conditions became milder and *Homo sapiens* learned to produce their own food directly from the ground, everything changed.

This Agricultural Revolution put an end to our need to live as nomads, wandering the planet in search of food supplies. Instead, small groups of humans became sedentary and started building small towns, then larger ones, then cities and even great civilizations. There were many benefits associated with this change, including the appearance of written language some five thousand years ago and the emergence of other disciplines, from mathematics to the beginnings of natural science, which helped promote a faster rate of progress.

Of course, this first human revolution demanded painful learning, too. Prior to the Agricultural Revolution, human beings organized themselves in groups or bands of around ten to fifty individuals, pretty much as chimpanzees still do.[30] This was a very loose, horizontal structure, with no formal authority granted to anyone. Older members of the group would be looked to for guidance and advice if needed, especially when problems arose, such as lack of food, external threats, or internal conflicts.[31] But life became more complicated in the agricultural era, when this small and simple form of organization was replaced by increasingly larger and more complex social structures, with castes, division of labor, formal rules, provision of common goods, and the like, created to deal with issues of power, order, justice, identity, freedom, rights, duties, and law. Eventually, this social evolution gave birth to large, hierarchical societies, beginning with the Middle Eastern empires of the Mesopotamians and Egyptians. In these societies, the only really important organization was the state itself, in the different forms it took over the centuries.

Several millennia after the Agricultural Revolution, a second revolution in the production system began. This was the Industrial Revolution of the eighteenth and nineteenth centuries, launched by the invention of new forms of energy that made different types of machinery possible, accelerating economic growth to levels never seen before. As a consequence, the shoemaker was replaced by the shoe factory, the stagecoach was replaced by the railroad company, the moneylender was replaced by the bank, the local candle provider was replaced by the electric company, the miner was replaced by the mining company, and so on and so forth. This economic transformation coincided with a number of fascinating and important political and social experiments — the first attempts to create large-scale societies based on democratic systems of governance.

Like the Agricultural Revolution before it, the Industrial Revolution produced both enormous benefits and painful challenges. It improved the quality of life for most of the world population and allowed millions to emerge from poverty, but it also demanded painful adaptations to a difficult transition: inequality grew among countries and people, raising a series of social questions and producing unprecedented levels of political turmoil, ideological conflicts, social unrest, and war.

Precisely when we were learning new ways of addressing some of these political and social challenges, as symbolized by the fall of the Berlin Wall in 1989 and the general acceptance of democratic capitalism as the best political/economic system on Earth, a third revolution in the means of production began to take shape. This was the Knowledge Revolution, which has been spreading at an incredible pace since the 1980s, making us face all sorts of adaptive challenges, systemically and individually. The source of this third revolution is the explosive mix of new modes of information and communication, whose best expression is the Internet. Never before has humanity been able to produce such vast amounts of knowledge and information, and make it accessible to anybody, at basically no cost.

The consequences of this change are enormous, starting with the empowerment of people. During the long era of hunting and gathering, individuals in a clan granted high status to the older members, whose experience was appreciated when new situations had to be faced. During the agricultural era, power and prestige shifted to those few who owned the land; they lived in relative comfort and ruled the society while almost everyone else had to work and live in miserable conditions. During the industrial era, the source of status shifted again: now the most valued people were the owners of capital, physical and financial, because this was now the scarce resource from which wealth and power flowed.

Today, in the knowledge era, capital is becoming steadily less scarce. Now power and prestige belong to those people who can make use of today's vast and widely accessible knowledge in ways that can add value to others. This includes millions of people, networking with partners through a laptop computer, a cell phone, or another type of electronic device. Suddenly the all-powerful resource that shapes the creation and sharing of wealth is one that is, at least potentially, universally accessible — knowledge itself and the ability to use it productively.

Entering an era dominated by this new entrepreneurial and creative power is a huge opportunity for organizations of all kinds — including nations themselves — but at the same time it poses a number of major adaptive challenges. Simply put, the type of organization that worked efficiently and effectively in the industrial era does not fit people living in the knowledge era. Organizations that do not realize this reality and act upon it will end up losing their most important asset — the knowledgeable people who are today's greatest future source of growth, wealth, and power.

It is said that the great twentieth-century industrialist Henry Ford used to complain, "Why is it that whenever I ask for a pair of hands, a brain comes attached?"[32] As harsh as these words may sound, they make perfect sense coming from a person who pioneered the assembly line with the goal of making automobile production as predictable, consistent, and mechanical as possible. By the end of the twentieth century, Jack Welch, the legendary CEO of General Electric, was describing the challenge of business leadership in very different terms: "The world is moving at such a pace that control has become a limitation. It slows you down. You've got to balance freedom with some control, but you've got to have more freedom than you ever dreamed of."[33]

These contrasting statements capture the crucial difference between the industrial era and the knowledge era. In the industrial era, the question was how to control employees so that they actually did what they were commanded to do, because their work was mostly technical, involving the repetition of actions that did not require new learning. In the knowledge era, the question is how to mobilize people so that they can make use of as much of their potential as possible. This is necessary because the type of work required to be competitive — the expression that we prefer to use nowadays instead of the traditional need to survive — is less technical and more adaptive, which means that more learning and less repetition is required.

The consequences of this change are enormous. Where the industrial organization was rigid, the knowledge organization is more flexible; where the former was pyramidal, the latter is more horizontal; where the former was command- and control-driven, the latter is more purpose- and culture-driven; where the former was focused on generating profits, the latter is more focused on generating value; where the former focused on workers' physical abilities, the latter focuses on workers' intellectual and emotional abilities; where the former considered people a necessary evil, the latter considers them more an indispensable asset; where the former was task-oriented, the latter is more relationship-oriented; where the former was linear-minded, the latter is more systemic-minded.

There's a well-known saying that reminds us: "If you keep doing the same thing, you will keep getting the same result." Yet, in an increasingly dynamic environment, the situation is actually worse than this: "If you keep doing the same thing, you will keep getting worse results." This is because there will be others who will improve their way of doing things, typically because they have a larger adaptive capacity.

Of course, as analyzed in Chapter 2, not all organizations face the same kind and level of adaptive challenges, but all of them need to constantly increase their adaptive capacity, even those that operate in industries that still recall the industrial era. If IBM and Telefonica had not increased their adaptive capacity, they might not exist anymore. The historical process that humankind has followed and that has been briefly depicted here simply reinforces this inescapable truth.

To succeed in this new world, you want as many people as possible experimenting with new strategies, new products, new teams, new systems, new processes, new alliances, new clients, new markets, and new assumptions. If employees are used to following the commands of their boss or the standard procedures, they will avoid thinking, acting, and taking responsibility when there is an opportunity for improvement or a problem that needs to be addressed. The result: a company that fails to take advantage of its potential, especially its people's capabilities. And this is a vicious cycle, because when that happens, the most talented people leave the organization, which means the company falls even further behind the competition.

LESSONS FROM EVOLUTION: FOCUS ON THE ADAPTIVE CHALLENGE

Modern *Homo sapiens* was not the first human being. This species appeared around 200,000 years ago, preceded by several other species of the genus *Homo*, which in turn evolved from the hominids or great apes. As environmental conditions changed and genetic recombination took place, some species disappeared and others emerged, preserving most of their ancestors' DNA and changing only a small part of it. In fact, when scientists compare the DNA of contemporary humans with that of chimpanzees, they find that about 99 percent is the same. Yet these seemingly small genetic changes produce enormous changes in body form, intellectual capabilities, and behavior.

Something similar happens with organizations. They too change over time, adapting to external conditions and needs through an evolutionary process that allows them to preserve what is essential, discard what is no longer required, and rearrange other aspects of themselves in order to better fulfill their goals. This evolution is a process of experimentation that looks for specific changes in what is expendable but potentially relevant, that tests variations and makes selections out of those variations based on their differing levels of success. And as with species, some organizations adapt and survive while others cease to exist because they are unable to face their adaptive challenges — that is, to change the small part of their DNA as needed to make them thrive.

However, there is an important difference between species and organizations as living systems. In biology, evolution is the result of a blind process of genetic variation, whereas organizational evolution is the result of a purposeful process of learning through experimentation. As environments change, it's inevitable that some species will disappear, because they do not have control over their process of genetic recombination. But organizations do have control over their learning process. When species adapt and survive, it is because of random chance; when organizations adapt and survive, it is because of the adaptive capacity they have developed through a deliberate act of leadership.[34]

The big challenge for organizations, then, is how to develop a larger adaptive capacity. This is not random — it is intentional. And it requires the exercise of leadership, first in asking what the organization needs to change, and second in mobilizing people toward that change. Making this happen requires discovering the adaptive challenge that underlies the problem.

Why is it that Saab Automobile could not adapt? Why is it that, instead of following the path that Audi or Volvo followed, it disappeared? It was a leadership failure, no doubt. But why did it become so difficult for the authorities at Saab to exercise leadership and make the organization adapt to a new reality, preserving its many strengths and changing what was needed?

The owners of Saab understood that they would not survive if they did not gain scale. Based on this awareness, they reached an agreement with GM in 1989. But did they realize the adaptive challenge that agreement implied? It was not just a matter of continuing to do the same things they'd always done while enjoying the financial backing of GM. Many elements of the old Saab needed to be preserved, but there were others that needed to be discarded. Experimentation to come up with new alternatives was critical, but that wouldn't happen without collaboration and innovation among engineers from the two different companies. That is where the adaptive challenge lay — but neither Saab nor GM fully recognized this, and therefore the challenge went unmet.

For two decades, teams from both companies subtly fought against each other, clinging to the different visions and values they held. They blamed each other for not being able to reach the established sale and production goals, using blame as a mechanism for avoiding their own part of responsibility and not activating themselves to do things differently. To make things worse, in 2003, after GM had taken full control of the company, 1,300 designers and engineers from Saab were laid off when the engineering department was merged with GM's European operations in Germany. This meant the end of Saab's ability to develop products with its own identity, and the beginning of its final extinction. The failure to recognize and respond to the company's adaptive challenge ultimately led to its demise.

By contrast, why was LATAM Airlines able to adapt and become an important actor in a highly competitive industry, in which many others disappeared? There was great leadership exercised by many executives, no doubt. But why was that possible? What are the specific aspects of this company that made it more adaptive than many others in its industry, allowing it to gain scale so successfully?

The key can be found in how the owners of LAN — the Chilean company's name before the merger — realized early on that the adaptive challenge they faced had to do with bringing in talent and opening up opportunities for its development. This need was not obvious in a Latin culture, where paternalism and dependency are more common than empowerment and accountability, nor was it obvious during the 1980s and '90s, when talent was scarce and more inclined to go to the financial sector than to a troubled industry like airlines. The Cuetos had to aggregate this talent-centric element to the DNA of the state-owned company they bought in 1994 as they discarded other elements of that DNA, such as cronyism and protectionism, which are characteristic of bureaucratic and communal organizations.

LAN was aggressive in hiring the best young professionals and opened room for people's initiative, creativity, and willingness to take advantage of the opportunities for improvement. This was true not only for executives, who would open a hub in Miami, for example, but also for crew members.

Instead of having a group of experts write a manual about onboard service for LAN's international flights — a key factor in the airline's strategy — managers decided to give that work back to a group of crew members, who worked together in developing a unique style that was passed on to all flights, assuring sustainability. As a result, the company has been recognized several times as the best Latin American airline and as the provider of the best on-board service in its commercial segment (Business Traveler, Skytrax, and Latin Trade). This openness to bottom-up innovation does not mean there is no control, especially if security protocols need to be fulfilled. It does mean that alignment depends less on top-down directives and more on the clear strategy and the strong culture that LAN Airlines started implicitly building early on, always allowing talent to develop within a flexible structure and with high levels of commitment.

By correctly defining and addressing its adaptive challenge, LAN Airlines developed a level of adaptive capacity that should allow it to thrive in the future, including passing the hard test imposed by the merger with TAM as well as the ultimate test it will face when the Cuetos no longer hold the key executive positions in LATAM Airlines.

Then there is the adaptive challenge faced by Telefonica. Was its adaptive capacity large enough to confront the reality imposed in the late '90s by changes in the telecommunications industry in Spain and its own privatization? Would the company be able to adapt as required to become a global player in the telecommunications industry and beyond?

As a state-controlled company with a monopoly over national and international telephone calls in Spain, Telefonica was a bureaucratic kind of organization for most of the twentieth century. Lacking competition, its environment was fairly stable and there was little need to focus on customers or other actors. And since the work tended to be more technical than adaptive, despite the technological advancements that occurred from time to time, there was little need to involve people in the decision-making process. In sum, Telefonica was an internally oriented and hierarchical organization, in which following the process was more important than attaining results, and in which people's main motive was safety. Despite the changes that had been taking place in the industry since the 1980s, in 1996, when Juan Villalonga was appointed chairman, it was still a paternalistic and slow-moving company.

To succeed when the announced deregulation came into effect, which meant competing in an open market, Telefonica had to face the big adaptive challenge of turning into a more dynamic and accomplishment-driven company — an action-driven kind of organization. Juan Villalonga understood this and put tremendous pressure to move the company in that direction, imposing a hectic rhythm that made Telefonica close most of the gap that separated it from other competitors in the industry. This effort certainly created lots of casualties, and many of those who were used to looking for safety ended up being replaced by others more oriented to accomplishing ambitious goals. As Telefonica's DNA changed, the disequilibrium that Villalonga created was so high that he himself became one of the casualties. It did not come as a surprise, therefore, that César Alierta cooled things down for a couple of years, even at the risk of losing competitiveness and letting the gap open again.

Villalonga moved Telefonica to the right in Figure 2-1, making it more externally oriented. Alierta moved it upward, which meant not only buying new companies and making challenging strategic decisions but also empowering members of the organization, providing more flexibility without losing control of key aspects of the business, and promoting innovation in certain departments. Given his background, it took Alierta some time to understand the new adaptive challenge the company faced to become a long-term global player in an increasingly complex, adaptive-oriented telecommunications industry. Moving fast was not enough. Nor was it enough to keep doing what they already knew how to do, even if their way was better than others. Telefonica had to discover what others had not discovered, which demanded experimentation and, most of all, a group of people highly driven to generate impact.

Ultimately, Alierta realized that to become an innovative kind of organization, Telefonica needed to create a new company, a spinoff that could preserve the best of its DNA while adding the levels of anticipation, creativity, collaboration, flexibility, and meaning that would be hard to develop within the mother ship.

This became Matthew Key's adaptive challenge. He assumed the call to create Telefonica Digital after the company's reorganization, led by Alierta in 2011, in an attempt to explore new terrain in the increasingly integrated world of information technologies and telecommunications. Indeed, the launch of Telefonica Digital meant taking a step beyond the industry of telecommunications, with an even larger adaptive capacity, in the hope that, sooner rather than later, Telefonica as a whole would follow that same path. Would this experiment work? Nobody really knew, but it was an interesting bet to take and a major adaptive challenge to assume.

It's worthwhile to compare Telefonica's evolution with that of HP. In a close-knit industry, Carly Fiorina tried to do something similar to what Alierta did with the creation of Telefonica Digital, but with HP as a whole. She understood that for the company to regain its leading position in electronic services, the adaptive challenge had to do with accelerating risk-taking. Much of the "HP Way" needed to be preserved, as the board emphasized, but comfort had gained too much space within the company, and that had to change. Yet Fiorina didn't fully understand how to make the organization face the adaptive challenge, especially in a scenario where HP's adaptive capacity was small in comparison to other players in the industry. Instead of mobilizing the organization to learn to take more risks, she took risks herself, making important business decisions in a more technical than adaptive mode. HP's adaptive capacity increased during Fiorina's tenure, but as a consequence of a rather traumatic process — one in which she herself became a casualty — rather than a well-designed plan. If Fiorina had fully grasped the nature of the adaptive challenge, the challenge itself would have stayed at the center of conversations, and business decisions would have followed, rather than vice versa.

IBM's Lou Gerstner understood this dynamic much better. The problem he faced was not merely about making business decisions only — though he made many — but about focusing people's attention on what they had to learn in order to meet the adaptive challenge. In the case of IBM during the 1990s, it all had to do with understanding customers' needs and making collaboration work. By focusing on this, Gerstner not only took care of the big problem IBM faced but also allowed the company to increase its adaptive capacity in order to better face the problems that would come in the future. He understood well that increasing an organization's adaptive capacity demands both conscious and purposeful work and a well-designed process.

LESSONS FROM EXPERIENCE: DESIGN A PROCESS

As we've seen throughout this book, adaptive work is difficult work. And when it takes the form of an organizational change, it can easily get out of hand and fail. As you have surely experienced yourself, in a process like this there is disequilibrium and tension, people perceive losses and react in varying ways, different factions emerge and take positions, uncertainty is rampant, plans fail, and experimentation becomes necessary. Guiding this type of process is highly demanding and requires a wide range of skills, especially from the CEO. In fact, leading adaptive work is likely to be the most important part of the CEO's job, as can be seen in most of the cases we have visited. Yet most top executives suffer these changes instead of guiding them, and even lose their jobs while trying to mobilize people along the way, as Carly Fiorina and Juan Villalonga did.

The larger the adaptive capacity of an organization, the easier it will be to lead these adaptive changes. And the more effective an organization becomes in carrying these changes out, correctly addressing the adaptive challenge, the larger its adaptive capacity will become. Once again, it's a virtuous cycle.

But for this to happen, the change process has to be thoughtful and well designed. Figure 3-1 shows some of the elements that this design should take into account, which will be explained in the following pages.

Figure 3-1. The design of a change process that increases adaptive capacity

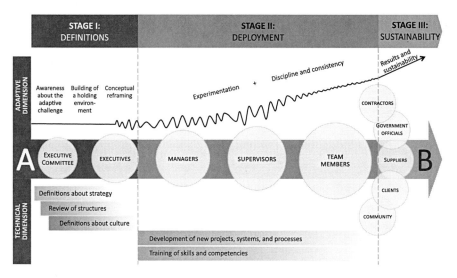

THREE STAGES IN THE CHANGE PROCESS

As we've discussed, change is always triggered by a problem, which is the gap between aspirations and reality. Organizational change can be triggered by situations like an economic downturn, a merger, a period of rapid growth, a need for innovation, new regulations, new competitors, expansion into new countries or markets, new controlling shareholders or executives, more Millennials joining the workforce, and so on. All of these can potentially be the source of a problem. It's easy to see how that is true with an economic downturn, but it can also be true when the company is growing. For example, the aspiration is to increase sales, but the reality may be that the plant isn't large enough to produce what is being demanded, or that the sales force is too small or lacks the competencies to sell more sophisticated products.

Whatever the trigger, there are three stages in the process of organizational change that will allow the company to move from one state of equilibrium (A) to another one (B), navigating through the disequilibrium zone, as shown in Figure 3-1:

1. Defining the challenge
2. Deploying the definitions
3. Achieving sustainability

Let's consider these three stages in turn.

The first stage of an organizational change process, defining the challenge, is what Gerstner did when he assumed power at IBM. Instead of making immediate decisions, he took quite a long time to observe the symptoms and interpret the plausible causes behind them. Together with his team, he reached the conclusion that the adaptive challenge IBM faced was focusing on its clients and collaborating among divisions to come up with integrated solutions. With that adaptive challenge clear — defined in terms of values, along the lines described in chapter 2 — executives could then come up with the concrete changes that they should carry out in regard to business strategy, structure, culture, systems, processes, and competencies.

César Alierta acted similarly at Telefonica. After a period of study and reflecting, he understood that, having grown as it had, the company's adaptive challenge was empowering people, providing more flexibility without losing control on key aspects. That allowed the board to make important definitions, among them the creation of Telefonica Digital, which would take innovation to a boundary the rest of the organization could hardly reach.

In this first stage, you want as many executives as possible to take part — including those on the board — to ensure that they will make those definitions their own in order to have the necessary context to carry out their implementation later on. Of course, it may be impossible to include too many people in the definitions stage, but a thoughtful design of this stage can allow for the sequential integration of many executives, at least those who constitute the critical mass that mobilizes the organization.

As part of the definitions stage, it is important to create a narrative that explains why this change is necessary and how it touches every person within the organization, connecting to people's values and emotions. This will be a powerful tool to help contain employees in the deployment stage, providing meaning in the midst of disequilibrium. And those who convey this narrative should include not only the CEO but many other executives. At IBM, for example, Gerstner was the main figure communicating the narrative, but he was joined by others, including Sam Palmisano, who had entered the company in 1973 as a salesman and would succeed Gerstner himself in 2002. I'll say more about the importance of narrative in chapter 4.

The second stage of an organizational change process is about deploying the definitions. If this were about technical work, the implementation of the prior definitions would be straightforward. People would simply apply their existing knowledge and know-how, making this a matter of pure execution. However, when adaptive work is involved, people may have to partially change their values, priorities, attitudes, or behaviors, which occurs neither automatically nor immediately. The deployment stage is precisely devoted to make this adaptive work take place. It will be easier if the organization has a large adaptive capacity when compared to the size of the adaptive challenge it faces, but it will still be difficult work and will still take time.

Fiorina never quite understood the need to tackle this kind of work within HP, though she did build a narrative to use as a communication resource for the process. The same thing happened with Villalonga at Telefonica; he put tremendous energy into expanding the business, but neglected the adaptive issues that would surely arise in that process. Neither Fiorina nor Villalonga gave people the chance to adapt, because they moved too fast and didn't pay attention to the losses they were generating among some factions within their companies and their boards. A well-designed deployment stage would have helped them survive and make the whole process more effective.

Seminars, workshops, training programs, special committees, flagship projects, coaching, spaces for courageous conversations, and other forms of communications support should accompany the deployment of the definitions and their internalization by employees, from executives to middle managers to supervisors and team members.

Finally, the third stage of an organizational change process is about achieving sustainability. In many change efforts, this is the most difficult stage of all, as people who have struggled with a weight problem know. Losing weight demands a lot of effort, often including the help of a nutritionist, a personal trainer, or even medical intervention. But it's a process that doesn't end when you reach your targeted weight. Attaining your visible goal doesn't mean that you've reached a new equilibrium. You're likely to still be in disequilibrium, tempted to return to your old eating habits or to stop visiting the gym. This means that the adaptive work is not finished yet and the effort must be maintained until the new habits you've adopted become natural or, in other words, become technical work. At that point, you've reached a new equilibrium and the lower weight you attained becomes sustainable.

The same happens with organizations. It takes time to integrate the new values, behaviors, competencies, practices, dynamics, processes, and systems. But once that is done, or mostly done, specific efforts must be devoted to sustain the change, making sure the new equilibrium has been reached. In this stage modeling becomes a critical factor. You want to have as many employees as possible consciously modeling the main traits that embody the change. In other words, you want a company filled with Palmisanos at all levels of the organization, not only speaking the narrative but also visibly acting in the new equilibrium mode, confronting others when they see something that's not in line with the new mode, mentoring promoted employees, leading new projects, facilitating workshops and training processes, and so on. Many anchors like these can help in sustaining what has been attained, and key employees must be ready to put those anchors in place. If this is done correctly, not only will the change be sustainable, but the organization will have increased its adaptive capacity.

And because organizations don't exist in a vacuum, external stakeholders must also be considered and involved in either the deployment stage or in the sustainability stage of the change process. These could include contractors, suppliers, clients, communities, government officials, customers, and anyone else who may be affected by the change. At some point you want them to do the part of the adaptive work that belongs to them, making change systemically sustainable.

FROM THE TECHNICAL DIMENSION TO THE ADAPTIVE DIMENSION OF CHANGE

As shown in Figure 3-1, the three-step process described has a technical dimension, but also an adaptive one. As we've noted, executives often face an organizational change by looking only at its technical aspects and ignoring its more critical adaptive ones. This would imply making definitions about strategy, structure, and culture in a room full of experts without looking at the losses that would result in internal and external stakeholders and the changes in mentality and behaviors that come with those definitions. It would also imply a deployment merely based on the development of new projects, systems, and processes, accompanied by courses or workshops aimed at training employees in specific skills and competencies. And there would be no real consciousness about the importance of involving executives, managers, supervisors, team members, and external stakeholders to make this change sustainable beyond the interests and pressure of those who initiated it. In simple terms, this would mean treating an adaptive challenge as a technical one, which would end up in failure or generate much more frustration and wasted effort than necessary.

David Franco made this mistake when he decided to buy a larger newspaper and a radio station in a nearby city. He made a strategic move, followed by some changes in the structure of the three companies, most of them related to the roles he would stop fulfilling at the *Home Star* and would assume in the newly acquired firms. But he didn't understand the impact those changes would have on people, some of whom would resent his absence and others who would resent his overwhelming presence. He just made decisions and continued acting in the way that was natural to him, without acknowledging the adaptive challenge his change had created, for others and for himself.

We've said that everything starts from a problem. When the problem has a technical nature, it's relatively easy to see and solve because it involves a solution that doesn't require a change in your thinking or behavior. But when the problem has an adaptive nature, it's difficult to see and solve because you're part of the problem and the solution calls for a personal change. The adaptive dimension of an organizational change is all about understanding what goes on with people during the process, helping them do the adaptive work that is required. And the first step is to make them aware that there is a problem and that they are part of the problem. If that step doesn't occur, people will remain where they are and change will not happen.

Moreover, people need to understand in what ways they will have to change, namely, what the adaptive challenge is. Employees at IBM and HP knew their company had a problem; recognizing this was just a matter of looking at the figures, especially at IBM. But Gerstner did a much better job than Fiorina of clearly framing the adaptive challenge underlying the problem, so that everyone in the company could be aware of the ways in which they were part of the problem and needed to change.

Making people aware of the adaptive challenge is the first step in this adaptive dimension of change, as shown in Figure 3-1. The second step is *building a holding environment*. The change process will need tension, which is the expression of the necessary disequilibrium. But if you don't want it to become destructive that tension needs to be contained. Thus it is important to make sure that the holding environment is strong enough for tension to be productive rather than destructive, and in the case of an organizational change that holding environment has to be gradually reinforced from the very beginning. Otherwise, bad news will be largely ignored, and those who are pushing change will run excessive risks.

This is what happened to Juan Villalonga at Telefonica. He didn't devote time to hold people in a process that seemed too hasty and threatening to most of them. The implicit message was that there wasn't anything of value in the past, and those who had been at Telefonica before didn't have anything to contribute to the splendid future that Villalonga envisioned for the company.

By contrast, when César Alierta succeeded Villalonga, he devoted two years to holding people together, hearing them, helping them feel necessary and valued, making sense of what was going on, opening spaces for participation, and pacing the work.

Of course change doesn't happen simply by holding people. It requires making them feel the tension that can lead them to move out of their comfort zone. Making them aware of the adaptive challenge was the first step in that direction, and making them realize the precise ways in which change will occur is the third step. We call this step *conceptual reframing*, and it has to do with adopting and cautiously conveying the definitions of what will be different in the future. It's a matter of strategy, structure, and culture, and it's important to let people understand that this is not an abstract exercise, but one that will come down to specific issues that will affect them. This is when employees start feeling the personal losses of the change process, and disequilibrium arises (if it wasn't already present), as it appears in the upper line of Figure 3-1.

David Franco never performed this work of conceptual reframing, which helps to explain some of the difficulties he encountered. By contrast, Lou Gerstner was a master at involving people in making these hard choices in connection with the adaptive challenge IBM had to face. Among many other changes that touched on people's direct interests, he modified the compensation structure, the rules for getting promotions, the product development process, and the dynamic of the business review meetings. By defining the changes in this concrete way, Gerstner made it possible for people to understand specifically how they needed to alter their own attitudes and behaviors.

When there is enough clarity about the path to be followed (which is always a matter of subjective definition, of course), concrete things have to start happening. This is the fourth step of the adaptive dimension, and I prefer to call it *experimentation* rather than implementation, because it's risky to see it as a perfect plan that only needs to be executed. You must never forget that the essence of adaptive work is learning, which by definition is about experimentation, that is, trial and error. Of course, you want as much success and as little error as possible, but it would be a mistake to assume that things must work well from the very beginning. When this false assumption is made and errors are committed, uncertainty rises and the informal authority of those who lead the change process falls, making things harder. It's wiser to talk about experimentation from the very beginning, and at the same time be disciplined and consistent in running those experiments in spite of some bad results that will most likely come up.

During the experimentation process, disequilibrium is likely to get to its highest level, and the temptation to go back or to detour to whatever comfort zone may appear is high as well. Telefonica Digital is an experiment in itself, born from the definition that Telefonica had to go beyond the traditional view of telecommunications and get immersed in the broader world of information technologies. That required the creation of different structures, values, and competencies, and instead of making the whole organization move in that direction — which would be too long and too difficult — running an experiment seemed to be more suitable. It was impossible to know in September of 2011, when Telefonica Digital was created, whether it would succeed, but they took the bet and carried out the experiment, basing the company in London and attempting to build a distinctive kind of culture, bringing highly qualified and innovative executives, and providing time to see whether it could work and show results.

How much time was appropriate? There is no straight answer to that, but Matthew Key knew that around the corner lay the impatience and the temptation of seeing this experiment through the eyes of the action-driven kind of organization that the parent company was. In fact, around the time of its second anniversary, Telefonica Digital had to make an important revision of its operating model, looking for more effectiveness and efficiency. In a letter titled "Time to Accelerate," Key explained this change to his people, concluding:

> We've been privileged to have been given a huge challenge by Telefonica — to create an amazing new business. We've risen to that challenge and made some great progress. We've continued to evolve our operating model and our revenues are accelerating. This must continue, or our leadership position in digital among the telcos will be jeopardized.... The key to any change of operating model is that we get through the period of uncertainty as quickly as possible — and continue to deliver the future while a period of uncertainty exists. This is particularly important at our stage of development.[35]

No doubt, these words showed that time was getting shorter and that the company needed to exhibit more concrete results soon. Four months later, on February 26, 2014, a major reorganization was announced by Telefonica's Board, aimed at giving "greater visibility to local operations, bringing them closer to the corporate decision-making center, simplifying the global structure and strengthening the transverse areas to improve flexibility and agility in decision makings."[36] This meant the end of Telefonica Digital, which was integrated, along with the European and Latin American business units, into a Global Corporate Center. Matthew Key, in turn, no longer held executive positions and remained as director of the British operation, leaving his seat as a member of Telefonica's board.

Was Telefonica Digital a successful experiment? It's not easy to tell. In the same official announcement, the board asserted that "Telefonica Digital has duplicated its value [since being formed] and has achieved incremental revenue to reach a growth of nearly 20 percent. In this way, it has become the seed for the Telefonica of the future." Moreover, the company used a blog to state that it is "more convinced than ever about the digital opportunity." On the other hand, some observers suggested that the closure of the digital unit indicated a lack of commitment to the path going forward.

So did Telefonica Digital help its parent company to increase its adaptive capacity — moving it upward in Figure 2-1, or did the parent company kill the son because it became a threat to the way Telefonica conceives itself? The decision adopted by the board must be seen in the end as the outcome of a struggle among factions that held different views about the experiment, some of them representing the more action-driven organization where Telefonica comes from and some representing the more innovative organization that Telefonica is eventually headed toward. What seems to be clear is that Telefonica Digital didn't deliver the results that some board members expected, and they decided to continue the experiment within the parent company. Only time will tell whether this was a decision that meant persevering with the challenge or avoiding it.

Achieving results, as shown in the case of Telefonica Digital, is critical, and it is the final step in this adaptive dimension of a change process. In the end, results make the change sustainable because they show that the effort and the disequilibrium were worthwhile. Before visible results appear, things are usually messy, with various factions emerging to battle for control of the organization.

Typically, we will see five different factions in a change process. The first are the mobilizers, those who struggle to overcome resistance, confronting people with the adaptive challenge that many others want to avoid.

A second faction are the supporters, those who favor the change because they see its benefits. Rather than taking on the risks the mobilizers assume, they prefer to stay in a safer place, supporting and applauding the mobilizers, but not exposing themselves.

A third faction, often the largest one, are the spectators, those who prefer to wait before they make up their minds; if things move along, they will join the effort, but if not, they stay behind.

A fourth faction are the skeptics, those who don't think the process will succeed and gossip all the time against it, saying that this is mistaken, efforts like this never work, the top executives don't know what they're doing, and so on.

Finally, a fifth faction is made up of the opponents, those who openly work against the process, taking the risks that come with this attitude because they perceive too important personal losses if change succeeds.

Basically, the adaptive dimension of the process is about mobilizing people from one faction to another, having as many mobilizers and supporters as possible, and as few opponents and skeptics as possible. Once there is a critical mass of people in the first group, spectators will move along and, little by little, change will start becoming a reality.

Here is where results play an important role, and quick wins need to be attained as soon as possible — especially the type of quick wins that will help you affect gain more mobilizers and supporters. Carly Fiorina obtained a quick win with the implementation of the previously approved separation of the company's technical equipment division into the stand-alone Agilent Technologies, but then she failed in her attempts to acquire PricewaterhouseCoopers' global management and information technology consulting business and the computer-services business EDS, efforts that were highly resisted by shareholders. The later merger with Compaq could have been seen as an important result of Fiorina's transformational intents, but it actually worked the other way around. For the main shareholders the merger was a sign of her stubbornness, which reinforced them as opponents, mobilizing powerful people into their faction until they were able to lay off Fiorina. Thus showing results is critical, though they must be intended to affect the balance among factions, increasing the number of mobilizers and supporters and decreasing the number of opponents and skeptics.

As we have seen, the adaptive dimension of a change process is crucial, and failure is almost always linked to having neglected this aspect of the process. It's not that the technical dimension is worthless, but it cannot be addressed without its adaptive component. You can draw a strategy in your own head or within a small group, just as you can figure out an organization chart, or define the values for the firm, or list the projects that will be carried out and the skills people need to have. But you will have created nothing more than a beautiful piece of paper that won't change anything if it is not accompanied by the more challenging adaptive dimension.

Here is an analogy: Suppose you have a severe back problem that is keeping you from running. Your doctor examines you, identifies the cause, and explains that you have to go to a kinesiologist five days a week for two months, change your posture, and practice yoga. This plan makes sense, but it demands that you change your priorities and behaviors, assuming some losses — which is why many patients fail to carry out their doctor's prescription.

The same thing happens with definitions about strategy, structure, and culture. The ideas may make a lot of sense, but they may also demand that people change their mentalities and behaviors. In both cases, an adaptive dimension requires awareness about the adaptive challenge, a holding environment to perform the adaptive work, reframing of ideas or visions, experimentation with discipline and consistency, and results that make change sustainable. If these elements are not present, lasting change will not occur. And of course in the case of an organization, the introduction of all these elements has to be done strategically, because there is a complex system in operation that will react in various ways.

SOME IMPORTANT CAVEATS

No two change processes are the same, but all share certain patterns. There is always disequilibrium and tension; people perceive losses and react; different factions emerge and take positions; there is uncertainty; it usually takes more time than expected; not everything works the way it was planned; and experimentation is necessary. This is why it makes sense to carry out a change process using a methodology like the one explained here, based on actual experience. Besides following the stages that have been described and always paying attention to the adaptive dimension, it is essential to be aware of certain aspects that are often skipped or understated in these situations.

First, those in authority must support the change process. Conceiving organizational changes implemented by mid-level managers is wishful thinking. Even though the need for change may start to spread from any part of the organization, it will not happen unless people with formal power get involved. Even in participative organizations, employees look to the authority figures in search of signals, especially when there is disequilibrium. If those signals don't express commitment, people will stay where they are. After all, why should they change and assume losses if the authorities don't do their part?

A change process must have a top-down design, as shown in Figure 3-1, at least within the boundaries of the division or department where it is taking place. For IBM to change, Lou Gerstner had to symbolize that change, not only modeling it in his personal behavior but also acting as its main mobilizer. Carly Fiorina also played this role, but she was never able to get the full board engaged, especially the founders' families, which distorted her message and let people get off the hook too easily.

Second, a change process can be led but not directed. This is because it is not linear, but systemic. It doesn't work by simply giving instructions and handbooks, because people have to learn and bear the losses attached to that learning. Therefore, they react in different ways and factions appear, not just once but several times, with each new stimulus.

Third, leadership of a change process must be a team effort. The more eyes and hands involved in conducting the process, the better, because there will be fewer blind spots and more mobilizing capacity. This is why a committee should be in charge of the change process, whether an executive committee or a special committee, but one with enough formal and informal power to get people's attention and involvement, and one with enough competencies to permanently diagnose and intervene. This is, in fact, the main purpose of central commands during battle, such as the U.S. Marines' experience in Nasiriyah shows. With many units involved and a lot of unexpected activity going on in the field, there was a need for a central team receiving information from various places and sources, interpreting it and designing broad or specific interventions.

Teamwork is also essential because change creates factions, including factions that oppose change and those that promote it. This means that leading a change effort is inherently risky, no matter how much enthusiasm, energy, and conviction you may have. Juan Villalonga had the enthusiasm, energy, and conviction needed to drive the tremendous expansion of Telefonica once it was privatized. And he succeeded in his effort, except that he could not enjoy the fruits of his success, because he was forced out. Had he devoted more time to building alliances with relevant people in other factions, inside and outside the company, the story might have been different.

The system — inside and outside the organization — tends to be stronger than you realize, and working with allies is good advice. The challenge is to devote time to establishing and reinforcing those alliances, making key people feel part of the process instead of making them feel like outsiders.

Fourth, one of the main sources of failure in change processes is treating them as mere communications campaigns. Adaptive change is about mobilizing people, not communicating ideas or facts to them. Executives often make decisions in a small group setting and then appeal to internal communications agencies to spread the word throughout the organization, assuming that alignment will happen almost automatically. This might work when it's mostly about technical work, but it's totally insufficient when it's mostly about adaptive work.

This is not to say that communications aren't important in a change process. They are — but only as support for the mobilizing effort, which requires a wider and more complex strategy, aiming at getting people out of their comfort zone. "One IBM" was not a communications campaign but rather the symbol of a very deep and hard process that made people seriously question the way they were working.

Fifth, a frequent mistake is launching a change process while failing to give value to what has been done in the past. If engineers at Saab had received an invigorating message about the wonderful cars they had built when GM started working with them, the story could have been different.

However, the subliminal message they heard from GM was that their cars were not good enough and everything had to change, starting with the chassis platform they were built on. When managers talk exclusively about the things that have to change, this is heard by people as if they didn't value what came before — that is, "they don't value me." This, of course, generates more resistance than needed and makes collaboration unlikely, as happened at Saab.

Finally, it's worth emphasizing that change requires determination. Executives often embark on a change process without the willingness to really produce an impact on people and create disequilibrium, assuming that employees will follow because the message is strong and the messenger is convincing. An illusion of change is created, and everyone talks about the importance of change, but no pain is actually felt. This is the illusion that Saab lived in for a decade after its 1989 agreement with GM. Besides the formal agreement, each team kept doing essentially the same tasks it had been doing on its own. The challenge of finding a GM-Saab way was never accomplished.

For real change to occur, the determination to create disequilibrium is critical, and so is the ability to sustain it, because adaptive change takes time. The lesson here is twofold: on one hand, be persevering, and on the other, think not only about the specific change the organization must address but also about how this change will help enlarge the organization's adaptive capacity for the long run.

This is what Lou Gerstner understood so well in his decade at IBM: his change effort wasn't only a strategic turnaround but a conscious effort at long-term adaptive capacity building. He strengthened the holding environment by infusing change with meaning, by providing context, by engaging people in conversations and decisions, by acknowledging their losses, by having change agents as allies, by leveraging partial results, by giving credit to the good things that had been done in the past, and by building trust in the system. He enhanced responsiveness by encouraging his people to hear the clients, by engaging his people in reflecting about what was going on outside and inside the organization, by making them feel responsible, by discouraging defensive behavior and silos, and by allowing smart risk-taking. The result: an IBM that is better equipped for any adaptive challenges tomorrow's world may pose.

DIFFICULT CONVERSATIONS: A BAROMETER OF ADAPTIVE CAPACITY

In Part Two of this book, we'll look at specific variables that affect an organization's ability to strengthen its holding environment and enhance its responsiveness. First, however, let's consider two behavioral signs that are useful initial barometers of a company's current adaptive capacity. The first of these is the way people in the organization face difficult conversations.

Saying things straight has never been easy. It demands courage and prudence from the speaker and openness from the listener. This particularly applies to what we call difficult conversations — the kind that arise when you know there is something that needs to be discussed but when the topic is such that you fear that the conversation may make things worse. It happens in marriage, among friends, and certainly within teams and organizations. We use the image of "the elephant in the room" to make this idea more tangible: people see it and feel its presence, but nobody wants to bring it up because they are afraid of what it may do.

Of course, we all know that the issues represented by the elephant must be discussed and that pretending they don't exist is an avoidance mechanism. Remember Jim, whose heavy-handed management style was alienating the engineers he supervised? What would have happened if Sarah hadn't told Jim that he was mistreating his people and invited him to have an open conversation with them? The faster difficult conversations are initiated, the better the likelihood that the problem will be solved and the organization will get unstuck.

Figure 3-2 shows the various ways in which these difficult conversations may be held. One way is to stick to a politically correct interaction, meaning that the issue is not addressed and everything remains the same. Another way is to provoke what we call a trenches debate, in which you overcome your fear and acknowledge the presence of the elephant but create a level of disequilibrium that pushes people into a defensive mode, looking to reaffirm their positions instead of trying to understand the challenge. A third way creates a reflective dialogue, in which the elephant is discussed but in such a mild way that no disequilibrium is created; the level of abstraction is too high, and people reflect on the issue as if they were not part of it. The fourth and final option is acknowledging the elephant in such a way as to create enough disequilibrium to make progress on the issue, producing a generative dialogue where people feel the tension yet remain engaged in the conversation.

Figure 3-2. Facing difficult conversations

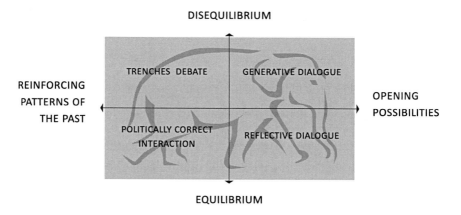

Moving people toward a generative dialogue requires a lot of individual competencies, but, most of all, it requires an environment that allows and even promotes difficult conversations. In regard to this trait, organizations differ widely — as do countries and cultures — and those that show a higher propensity to generative dialogue typically exhibit a larger adaptive capacity. Observing a team's or an organization's ability to move quickly toward generative dialogue when there is an elephant or elephants in the room is a simple and effective proxy for analyzing its adaptive capacity.

LAN Airlines is an example of an organization in which people say things straight, producing generative dialogue rather than defensive reactions. This trait was brought to the organization by the founding Cuetos and became an unspoken part of its DNA. This was not the case at TAM Airlines, where people were used to a more oblique type of dialogue. Difficult issues were not discussed explicitly but implicitly, producing misinterpretations, confusion, indecisiveness, and hesitation. This important cultural difference has made the merger of the two airlines more difficult than expected. The problem is exacerbated by the fact that the two companies speak different national languages — Spanish and Portuguese — which of course is a relevant factor in ease of communication across company boundaries.

HOW THE AUTHORITY FACES ADAPTIVE CHALLENGES: A SECOND BAROMETER

A second useful barometer of an organization's adaptive capacity is the way in which authority is exercised. In general, the behavior of the person in authority mirrors the system, because she is there to satisfy people's expectations; if she behaves in a way that is too different from the way the system behaves, she will be expelled by it.

Figure 3-3 shows four ways in which authority can be exercised, according to each kind of organization we described in Figure 2-1.

In an action-driven organization, authority will typically be exercised in a directive way, making decisions and giving orders that will make people and things move fast and accomplish results. This approach usually functions pretty well, because most of the work is technical and there is a need to permanently and quickly cope with an unstable environment.

In a bureaucratic organization, authority will typically be exercised in a paternalistic way, by assuming responsibility and making people feel safe. This approach is generally effective because most of the work is technical and there is no need to make fast decisions given the stability of the environment.

In a communal organization, authority will typically be exercised in a conciliatory way, by reinforcing the sense of belonging by making everyone feel included and heard, no matter how much time that takes. This usually functions well, because adaptive work is carried out by making people participate in decisions and, given the stability of the environment, there is no need to move fast.

Finally, in innovative organizations, authority will typically be exercised in a facilitative way, by providing space and resources for people to deploy themselves and generate impact. This normally functions well, because people assume responsibility, generating an environment of horizontal collaboration and learning that promotes adaptive work in a way that allows the organization to cope with the unstable environment it lives in.

Figure 3-3. Four ways of exercising authority

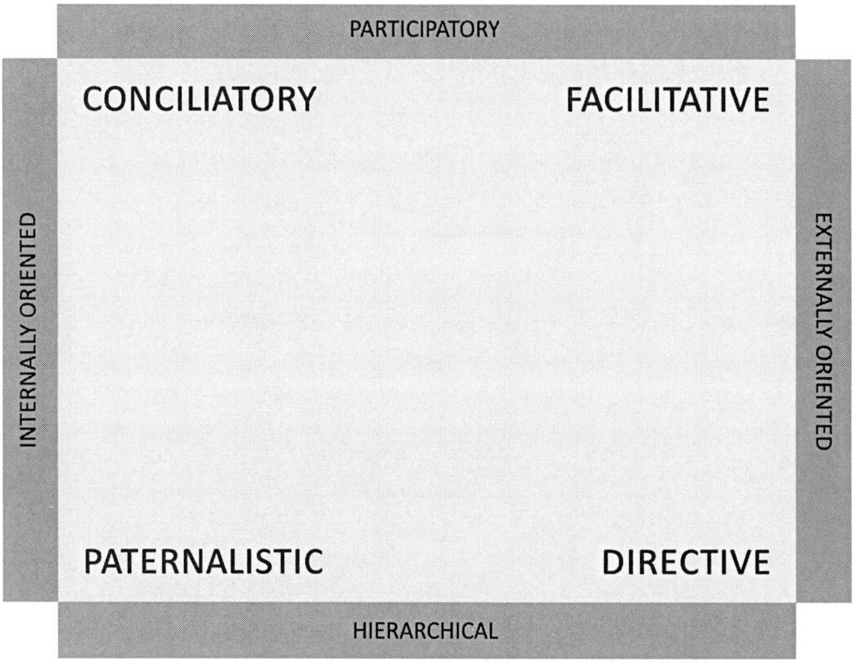

Observing the mode in which the authority is exercised in an organization is a simple and effective proxy for analyzing its adaptive capacity. For example, when an authority can operate in a facilitative mode, it's because the organization's adaptive capacity is large. On the other extreme, when the authority has to be paternalistic, it's because the organization's adaptive capacity is rather small.

This means that increasing the organization's adaptive capacity poses a challenge for authorities, because they will have to operate in a way that creates some level of disequilibrium. In a bureaucratic organization, for example, people want the authority to be paternalistic; but if he wants to increase the collective adaptive capacity, he will have to become more directive, to a degree that is noticeable but not excessively disruptive. The same is true for a conciliatory way of exercising authority in a communal organization; the authority will have to integrate some facilitative traits, giving the work back to people to make them responsible even if they feel uncomfortable with that. And in the case of an action-driven organization, in which people are used to a more directive mode of exercising authority, increasing the adaptive capacity will demand facilitating spaces for people to use their creativity and come up with their own ideas and solutions, even if they prefer to follow orders, which is what they are used to. In all these cases, of course, authorities face their own adaptive challenge in acting in a different way than the one they're used to, which tests their individual adaptive capacity.

Telefonica exemplifies the way in which the exercise of authority has evolved over time. When it was a state-owned company, authority was exercised in a paternalistic mode, which made a lot of sense for a bureaucratic kind of organization. Once privatized, Telefonica could no longer remain in that condition, because it now had to operate in a competitive market. Accordingly, CEO Juan Villalonga exercised his authority in a highly directive mode, mobilizing the organization to be less bureaucratic and more action-driven. However, he moved too fast, creating a gap between himself and the organization, which led to his dismissal.

Villalonga's successor, César Alierta, reduced the pace for a while. After a while, Alierta realized that Telefonica could not be a purely action-driven organization, because the industry was walking toward higher degrees of innovation and dynamism, which meant that talent had to play a more important role than before. He introduced some facilitative traits into his role, but to a limit imposed by his own competencies and the reality of the big organization he was heading. However, because he knew that at least part of the organization needed to become innovative without waiting a decade, Telefonica Digital was born, with a CEO in Matthew Key who clearly exercised his authority in a facilitative mode, modeling the innovative kind of organization that was needed.

The ideas presented in this chapter show that increasing an organization's adaptive capacity should not be left to randomness. On the contrary, increasing adaptive capacity should be a conscious process, addressed as part of specific business challenges the organization has to confront to continue thriving, or addressed as an organizational challenge on its own. Either way, defining the underlying adaptive challenge and designing a process to meet it are two key elements required to move forward. If this is thoughtfully done, a virtuous cycle is created, in which the more adaptive work the organization performs, the more its adaptive capacity will increase.

In this first part of this book, key questions were asked that you need to answer to understand what adaptive capacity is about. Chapter 1 analyzed why organizations tend to remain in equilibrium and how that can be altered, increasing the adaptive capacity to face problems and change. Chapter 2 introduced four kinds of organizations — action-driven, bureaucratic, communal, and innovative — each of which requires a different level of adaptive capacity to confront its problems, but all of them facing the challenge of becoming more adaptive. Chapter 3 explained how to become more adaptive when you see the adaptive challenge that hides behind the problem and design a process to tackle it.

With this background, you should be now equipped to address the first three of the four questions about your organization, which were presented in the Prologue:

- How much adaptive capacity does it have?
- Is that adaptive capacity enough to meet the challenges it faces?
- How can its adaptive capacity be increased?
- What are the variables that may increase its adaptive capacity?

The second part of the book addresses the fourth question. I'll explain how your company can increase its adaptive capacity by touching on concrete and practical variables connected to its adaptive challenge. Whether small or large, a gap between your company's current adaptive capacity and its ideal capacity will always exist, meaning that you should never stop thinking of ways to become more adaptive. The variables I'll discuss are aimed at helping top executives focus their attention and the efforts to better address this never-ending challenge.

Of course, the quest to make an organization more adaptive is not an exact science and there is no magical number of variables involved. Nonetheless, based on my experience in studying companies and working with them, I will refer to 25 variables, grouped in the following five dimensions, which provide a comprehensive view of an organization.

Since a social system mirrors the way a biological system functions, it is useful to draw a parallel with specific elements of the human body:

- Purpose — the organization's soul
- Strategy — the organization's brain
- Structure — the organization's skeleton
- Culture — the organization's blood
- Talent — the organization's heart

PART TWO

HOW TO INCREASE
AN ORGANIZATION'S
ADAPTIVE CAPACITY

In the fourth century BC, Aristotle said, "The whole is more than the sum of its parts."[37] This statement is as applicable to the universe as it is to an organization, an engine, or the human body.

Behind these words lies the holistic concept of reality, meaning that everything is an element in a larger system whose different parts are all connected to one another and affected by one another. When the focus is put on specific parts only, the big picture is lost and comprehension of the whole is limited.

Taking a holistic view of their organizations is one of the main challenges executives face, given that every single person has certain default settings and blind spots that drive him or her to see only a part of the picture.

The five organizational dimensions that will be the subject of the following five chapters help provide that holistic view. At the same time, these dimensions allow us to dissect the whole into a series of separate parts, enabling us to intervene where necessary while never losing sight of the connections among the dimensions.

Based on these premises, we will address the following issues in this half of the book:

- How can an organization be divided into a set of dimensions that will make it easier for us to get a complete analytical view of its workings?
- What variables in each dimension have a direct impact on the organization's adaptive capacity?
- How will those variables appear in each of the four kinds of adaptive organizations?

- What mechanisms do organizations use to avoid making progress on those variables? And how can these avoidance mechanisms be counteracted, making progress possible?

By the time you finish reading Part Two, you should be able to answer these questions, especially in regard to your own organization. This, in turn, should equip you to begin the process of increasing your organization's adaptive capacity, thereby making it better equipped to cope with the adaptive challenges it is sure to face in the years to come.

CHAPTER 4

PURPOSE:
THE ORGANIZATION'S SOUL

If people in your organization are not motivated to give their best, you have a problem. And that problem is likely connected to a lack or shortage of purpose.

Biologically speaking, the soul is not part of the human body, yet it is the central aspect of the human being. The soul can be understood as the quest for an answer to why we exist, what our purpose in life is. The concept of purpose plays the same role in an organization.

Human life is more than doing things; it is even more than doing things well. Life is about meaning, and for thousands of years humans have connected the quest for meaning to the concept of a transcendent value — one that will outlast our limited life span here on Earth. The most obvious, visible way to embody that sense of transcendent value is through having descendants, but it is certainly not the only one. Over time humans have increasingly explored other ways of leaving a transcendent legacy behind, including social or political traditions, ideas, books, discoveries, buildings, inventions, organizations, public policies, and institutions, just to name a few.

When basic survival needs are met, which is becoming the case for more and more people, especially in developed countries, psychological needs such as the desire for transcendent value take center stage. This shift has a profound impact on our relationship with work. Work is no longer a matter of merely exchanging services for money, it is also an opportunity for fulfilling a higher personal purpose; work is not only about making a living, but also about making history; work is not only about doing well, but also doing good. In short, work is all about having a lasting and positive impact on the world.

For this reason, an organization without a purpose will not be able to attract people who work with purpose. It will look like an industrial type of organization, focused exclusively on performing tasks in an efficient way, treating people as mere executors of corporate plans rather than unleashing their full potential. By contrast, an organization with purpose will go beyond the task, understanding that its main asset is people who work with purpose and seek to make a difference, both as individuals and as members of the organization. An organization without purpose manages human resources, whereas an organization with purpose mobilizes people.

GRAMEEN BANK, AVON, APPLE: THREE VERY DIFFERENT ORGANIZATIONS DRIVEN BY PURPOSE

The Grameen Bank, a microfinance institution founded in Bangladesh in the late 1970s by economist Muhammad Yunus, is a good example of a purpose-driven organization. As with any other bank, the task of Grameen Bank is to lend out money and collect the capital and interest over time, earning a profit. But in this case, there was a deeper purpose beyond that task: community development. The target market of Grameen Bank is poor women in rural areas, who have no access to traditional credit with which to finance their small business initiatives. Yunus realized that by lending small amounts of money to groups of women in a community, making all of them accountable for each other's debt, they would grow their projects, pay back the loans, and contribute to the development of their communities.

The microcredit model developed by Yunus has been exported to many other developing countries all over the world and has also been expanded to other development-oriented businesses, such as telephone and energy companies. People who work in these organizations receive a competitive salary, but their motivation goes beyond material rewards, because they realize they are making a difference. They are there because of a personal purpose, which is connected to the organization's purpose. The impact of

Yunus' idea has been so great that, in 2006, he and Grameen Bank were jointly awarded the Nobel Peace Prize.

Grameen Bank does not exist primarily for the purpose of growing its profits. But even companies driven by the profit motive can also have a larger underlying purpose. The cosmetics company Avon is an interesting case of a business organization with a clear purpose, in which there is an outcome beyond the financial output. The business itself is about producing and selling cosmetics, fragrances, and toiletries, but there is also a larger purpose embedded in Avon's business design. Since its origins in 1886, Avon's business model has been based on a door-to-door sales approach, performed by women acting as independent sales representatives, who could combine their role as homemakers with that of working women making a salary and enjoying the enhanced freedom and prestige associated with being breadwinners.

In 1999, Andrea Young became the first woman to reach the position of CEO at Avon. She immediately constructed a narrative to provide meaning to the work that Avon's employees had been doing for more than a century, work whose inspirational quality had not been sufficiently exploited. Young noted, "In 2000 we adopted our vision statement, 'The Company for Women.' What we do is to elevate women in the community. We create commerce that can better their families' lives, particularly in emerging markets. It is purposeful work. I don't believe that shareholders have it at the top of the list of objectives in most public companies."[38]

It is one thing to wake up in the morning and go to work for a company that sells cosmetics in order to maximize shareholder value; it is quite another to do the same work for the sake of women's empowerment and progress. And it should not come as a surprise that when Young left her position in 2012 to become Avon's executive president, her successor was also a woman.

Here is another example from a very different industry. Steve Jobs, the founder of Apple, lived his life with an intense focus on the purpose of his work. "Being the richest man in the cemetery doesn't matter to me," he once said. "Going to bed at night knowing we've done something wonderful — that's what matters to me." And this personal purpose was embodied in Apple. "My passion has been to build an enduring company where people were motivated to make great products. Everything else was secondary. Sure, it was great to make a profit, because that was what allowed you to make great products. But the products, not the profits, were the motivation."[39]

Things changed for Apple in 1983. John Sculley, former president of PepsiCo, was appointed Apple's CEO by the board. The move quickly generated a power struggle between Sculley and Jobs, ending in Jobs' removal from his managerial duties in 1985. Sculley himself was forced out in 1993, after sales, margins, and stock price had eroded. The difference between a company driven by purpose rather than profits turned out to be crucial to Apple's success. "It's a subtle difference," Jobs said, "but it ends up meaning everything — the people you hire, who gets promoted, what you discuss in meetings."[40] Jobs returned to the leadership of Apple, and the company resumed its role as a leader in the world of high-tech innovation.

Every organization, whether small or large, for profit or not for profit, in industry A or industry Z, can have a purpose with an impact beyond the products or services it produces. In simple words, you can be cutting stones or building a cathedral, it's your choice, but the choice makes a vast difference for yourself and those who work for you — as the story of Apple's ups and downs illustrates.

In those organizations that have a purpose, people are motivated to give their best, they want to remain there and collaborate with others to be as impactful as possible, and they understand that the task they are performing is connected to a larger meaning. This is certainly inspiring, especially for the current generation of young workers, who have been shown by numerous surveys and studies to be particularly idealistic and purpose-driven in their attitudes toward work. At the same time, purpose builds a very strong holding environment, thereby helping to increase the adaptive capacity of the organization and its readiness to surmount unexpected challenges.

Thus there's a strong connection between having a purpose and being more adaptive. Let's put it this way: people with purpose do not get trapped in the comfort or the difficulties of the status quo; when adaptive challenges arise, they will find their way to make a difference, challenging themselves to change and thrive as circumstances require. Organizations with purpose will do the same, because they believe that the outcome is far more important than the current output, structure, standard operating procedures, or practices. In truth, there is nothing more powerful than purpose to align people.

FIVE KEY VARIABLES: DIFFERENCE, PEOPLE WITH PURPOSE, LEGACY, CONNECTION, NARRATIVE

Within the dimension of purpose are five key variables you need to think about and measure in pursuing greater adaptive capacity:

1. *The difference* the organization makes in the world
2. The practice of hiring *people with purpose.*
3. *The organization as a legacy*
4. The organization's *connection with the community*
5. *An overarching narrative*

If we go back to Figure 1-1, these variables can increase your organization's adaptive capacity by strengthening the holding environment, enhancing the responsiveness, or both. Let's consider them one by one.

The difference. Most people start a business as a way of making money, be it for survival or for covering other less obvious needs, like power, recognition, or autonomy, just to mention a few. Since this is the typically assumed answer to the question "Why we are doing this business?" the question is rarely explicitly asked. Instead, we generally focus on asking what we will do to make money — or maximize profits, in economic terms — and how we will do it.[41]

But Steve Jobs, Muhammad Yunus, Andrea Young, and many others have taken a different approach. They all started by asking themselves and their closest associates *why* they wanted to get involved in a particular business. Making money was part of the answer, of course, but not the most relevant one — not the one that would motivate them to dedicate their time, energy, resources, and lives to the business.

Making a difference is connected to the aspiration of having an impact on others, of building something larger than oneself. That means having a purpose, which should exist not only in the souls of the founders but with hope in the souls of every employee. If that is the case, people will not be merely performing tasks but collaborating with their colleagues in making a difference to those who will buy their products and services, and making a profit will be the consequence.

Making a difference, therefore, will increase the organization's adaptive capacity mainly by strengthening the holding environment, because people will want to be part of a group that is improving the lives of others.

When thinking about your own organization, ask yourself, "Do our executives talk about why we do what we do?" and "Do people in our company realize the difference we are making to others and take pride in it?"

People with purpose. Just as there are boards and top executives who see only the bottom line of financial statements, there are employees who see only the dollar amount on their monthly pay check. These people work for a company to perform a task in exchange for a salary, like most people working for companies since the beginning of the Industrial Revolution.

Today, however, these transactional work relationships are being replaced by what we could call "engaging relationships." Millennials in particular are moving the boundary here, as a cohort made up largely of people who join companies to make a difference rather than perform tasks in exchange for a salary.

A company increases its adaptive capacity when it hires people who have a purpose, which in turn is connected to the organization's purpose, especially in positions that involve a higher percentage of adaptive work. These are individuals who will always be challenging themselves and the organization, making it thrive. It is easier, of course, to manage people who are not moved by a purpose and who limit themselves to follow instructions and rules. But this approach to work serves only to maintain the status quo rather than increase the organization's adaptive capacity. On the contrary, having people with purpose will enhance the organization's responsiveness, making it more adaptive, because purpose-driven individuals are always looking for more challenges.

When thinking about your own organization, ask yourself, "How relevant is learning about applicants' purposes and their connections to the company's purpose in our employee selection process?" and "What kind of conversations do bosses have with each member of their teams in regard to purpose, and how is that information used in opening opportunities to people?"

The organization as a legacy. Steve Jobs' legacy was not the Macintosh, the iPod, the iPad, or any of the other high-tech devices he created.

In his own words, his legacy was Apple, the organization. It's possible that other business founders, from LAN Airlines' Enrique Cueto to HP's Bill Hewlett and Dave Packard, might feel the same about the companies they built. But not all founders have this kind of mentality, and there are many, in fact, who create companies with the sole goal of selling them quickly for as much money as possible.

Similarly, there are CEOs who think about the kind of enduring organization they want to pass on to their successor — as Lou Gerstner did at IBM and Jack Welch did at GE — while others run companies thinking mainly about the short-run financial return. We could apply the same distinction to any person who heads a team within a company, who could be thinking about building a sustainable team that can outlive her or about producing short-term results to get rapidly promoted. The key word here is *sustainability*, which is inherently connected to purpose and adaptability, at the organization, the team, and the individual levels.

Promoting sustainability is a way of increasing the organization's adaptive capacity by strengthening its holding environment, because people want to be part of a lasting effort — one that constitutes a legacy to future generations.

When thinking about your own organization, ask yourself, "How much time do top executives devote to organizational development?" and "How ingrained in the company's language is the word *sustainability*?"

Connection with the community. People do not live alone, and neither do organizations. As individuals, we are part of a family, of a team, and of larger systems such as an institution, a region, or a nation. Organizations, in turn, are part of a community, which may be as small as a little town or as big as the entire world. Both individuals and organizations have to strive to live in harmony with others, building and participating in an ecosystem in which they and others can survive, thrive, and grow.

This means that purposeful work is not only about fulfilling our own purposes as individuals or organizations, but also about allowing — and even helping — others to fulfill their purposes, whether or not these are parallel to or supportive of our own.

In some industries, the importance of forging strong, positive relationships with the community is inescapable. This applies to companies extracting natural resources, for example, since the communities that are close to the exploitation places (such as mines, oil wells, or factory farms) are increasingly demanding attention to their own needs and ideals. Companies now have to work hand in hand with their neighbors to receive the social authorization to go ahead with their projects.

But this principle doesn't just apply to natural resource companies, nor is it simply a matter of compensating for damage that may be done by a business to the communities in which it operates. Telefonica, for example, has a foundation that, among other things, provides broadband and educational resources to public schools, because it understands that even though the company produces no evident damage to people or the environment, citizens expect it to be a good citizen, too. The same level of consciousness is present in an increasing number of companies, which try to connect to other purposes in the community, becoming aware of new realities and adapting as necessary, and thereby gaining and regaining social authorization.

This connection with the community will increase the organization's adaptive capacity by both strengthening the holding environment and enhancing its responsiveness. The more ties that exist — internal and external — the more people feel held; and the more you consider other voices in the community, the more responsive you yourself become.

When thinking about your own organization, ask yourself, "Do we take into account what citizens — not simply customers or clients — think about us?" and "What do we do to understand and get connected to other purposes in the community or communities we are related to?"

An overarching narrative. "So even though we face the difficulties of today and tomorrow, I still have a dream. It is a dream deeply rooted in the American dream. I have a dream that one day this nation will rise up and live out the true meaning of its creed: 'We hold these truths to be self-evident; that all men are created equal.'"

A narrative is a story built upon a purpose — ideally a purpose that is able to touch people's hearts and strings because it connects to their own values. Martin Luther King Jr.'s "I Have a Dream" address, delivered from the Lincoln Memorial before a vast audience of civil rights marchers in 1963, is one of the best examples of a well-constructed narrative. King was able to connect his own story and the story of African Americans with the story of all Americans: "It is a dream deeply rooted in the American dream."

The purpose of narrative is more emotional than rational, more in the realm of meanings than realities, and more about inspiration than persuasion. This is why it cannot be conveyed through a routine or purely factual speech, as the delivery of your company's quarterly or annual results would be.

The purpose must be part of an overarching narrative, one in which the story of the company gets connected to the story of the people who work in the company and the story of the storyteller, all tied up by shared values.

Politicians and activists know a lot about this because they have to engage and reengage people all the time. By contrast, most executives think that paying a salary should suffice to hold people. That may have been true at one time, but in today's world, where engaging and retaining the most committed and creative employees is a crucial challenge for every business, inspiring your people through a purpose-driven narrative is an essential skill for every manager.

A narrative is able to increase an organization's adaptive capacity by both strengthening the holding environment and enhancing its responsiveness. The holding environment is strengthened by the shared values upon which the narrative is built, and responsiveness is enhanced because the narrative helps to make people aware of the challenges they face.

When thinking about your own organization, ask yourself, "Have we built a narrative that allows people to connect their motives to the company's purpose?" and "Do our top executives use that narrative as a way to engage and energize our people?"

PURPOSE IN VARIOUS KINDS OF ORGANIZATIONS

It is certainly easier for a church to have a purpose than it is for a car manufacturer. Whereas churches build their message upon the idea of transcendent value, which as we've seen is at the core of purpose, car manufacturers devote most of their resources to the massive production of those transportation devices called automobiles. The same is true if we were to compare an NGO with an investment bank, a university with a printing firm, or a high-tech company with an oil producer. This last-named case may seem less obvious than the others, but let's consider it. A high-tech company generally dedicates its resources to developing brand-new products and services that expand human capabilities, enhance creativity, and enable new connections among people. This focus makes it relatively easy for a high-tech company to define its purpose in a way that connects with transcendent values. By contrast, an oil producer is simply extracting a limited resource from the earth for use in processes defined by others — running factories, powering automobiles, and so on. It's a worthy activity, but it has a less direct link to any transcendent value.

This means that some industries are more suited than others to having a stronger purpose. But it is also true that even within a particular industry we will find companies that do a better job than others in building a sense of purpose. It is just a matter of comparing, for example, Apple with HP, Grameen Bank with Citibank, or Avon with Maybelline.

It would be difficult for an investment bank to do purposeful work as an NGO does. It would demand changing its nature. But it could certainly try to make progress in this dimension, which would help it increase its adaptive capacity.

How much progress in this direction might your company attain to become more adaptive? To answer this question, go back to Figure 2-2 and use the kind of organization your industry is closest to as a benchmark. Generally speaking, we should expect communal and innovative organizations to have a stronger purpose than bureaucratic and action-driven organizations, since they do more adaptive than technical work and therefore are more participatory and less hierarchical. As a result, people are their main focus and asset, including both those who work for the company as well as those who are outside but connected to it.

As an example, Apple produces technological devices and does so in a way that transcends the purely mechanical. When its engineers design those devices, they are thinking about the people who will use them and striving to have an impact that will make a difference in their lives. At the same time, those who run Apple and head teams within it know that if they want to make a difference as a company, their main focus must be on unleashing their own employees' potential. It is this connectivity among human beings that makes work meaningful. It is also the reason communal and innovative organizations naturally tend to have a stronger purpose than bureaucratic and action-driven organizations, which are more product- or service-oriented than people-oriented.

To be more specific, let's look at the five variables related to the purpose dimension and see how they might look like for each kind of organization. The results can serve as a benchmark for your own company, depending on the kind of organization it is closest to. You may find it helpful to think about the corresponding five variables as the knobs of a music equalizer, as shown in Figure 4-1. Just as a song can be heard differently, depending on how those knobs are set, the performance of a company will be different, depending on how those variables are set. If you want to change your company's performance and increase its adaptive capacity, some of those organizational knobs might have to be adjusted. It's certainly harder than moving the knobs of a music equalizer, but attainable when consciously worked through, following a process like the one depicted in Chapter 3.

Figure 4-1. The purpose equalizer

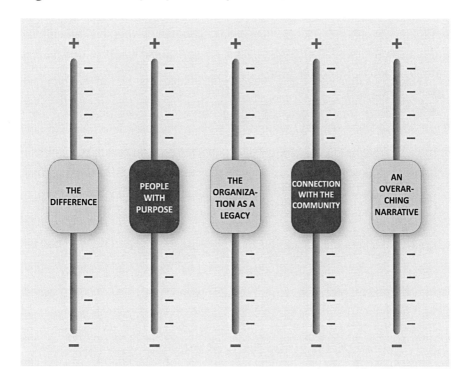

When thinking about a communal organization — a public school, for instance — the five knobs of the "purpose equalizer" should be in the upper range. If that is not the case for your own organization — if it is of the communal kind — it means there is a gap with the potential to be addressed.

For an innovative organization — an advertising agency, for instance — the potential to raise the knobs to the upper range is there, but it is less natural than for a communal organization. This is because market pressures can make people within an innovative company move too fast, losing perspective and forgetting about their job's meaning and purpose. There is certainly the potential for an innovative organization to make a difference, bringing in people with purpose, making organizational development an important focus, finding connections with other purposes in the community, and wrapping everything up in a powerful narrative. But the leadership of the company is paramount in attaining this. Although Steve Jobs was able to do it, Carly Fiorina did not.

In the case of bureaucratic and action-driven organizations, we would not expect to see any of the knobs above the middle range of the equalizer. Nevertheless, because many bureaucratic organizations are related to civil service — the judiciary, for instance — a reason for existing could be an element used in inspiring people, especially as part of a narrative built for an organizational change process. Other exceptions can also be imagined. LAN Airlines, for example, is an action-driven organization that has been able to keep the five knobs in the middle range or even higher despite the nature of its work. This is largely due to being a company that initially made people proud of succeeding far beyond the frontiers of the small country where it was founded, Chile, an element that has gradually faded away with the company's international nature, especially after the merger with TAM Airlines.

Perhaps because it is essential to human nature, purpose is always latent in a social system, waiting to be articulated and lived. Nonetheless, experience shows that this is easier in certain kinds of organizations than it is in others.

HOW COMPANIES AVOID THE ISSUE OF PURPOSE, AND THE POWER OF ASKING "WHY?"

Just as it is difficult to find doctors trained in traditional Western medicine talking about the soul, it is equally difficult to find business managers talking about purpose. For most physicians, the "soul" has nothing to do with the practice of medicine; likewise, for most traditional managers, "purpose" has little to do with business.

People like Steve Jobs, Muhammad Yunus, and Andrea Young have personal traits that might make us think they are outsiders in the business community. Jobs was always a rebel, who did as much as he could to challenge traditional business thinking. Yunus came from academia and has been strongly related to the not-for-profit sector. And Young is a woman, preceded by a succession of men in the positions of CEO and president of Avon.

For all three of these personalities, acting with purpose was paramount in their lives, so inspiring others came naturally to them. Conversations with them, therefore, could be expected to be more people-oriented than task-oriented. They were motivated — and in the case of Yunus and Young still motivated — by having an impact on others and leaving a legacy behind.

More traditional managers find their comfort zone in talking about tasks and results. Those are concrete things that can be discussed in rational, objective terms. They talk about what to do and how to do it, but not about *why* it should be done.

What we see operating in the typical manager is an avoidance mechanism, a self-defensive process that allows him to stay in his comfort zone without experiencing the need to move to another space, in this case the purpose space. Generally speaking, an avoidance mechanism, which can operate either at a conscious or an unconscious level, is activated by the fear of losing something. In the case of purpose, it would usually be the loss of credibility.

Purpose has a lot to do with connecting with others at the emotional level using the right hemisphere of the brain — metaphorically speaking — a skill few executives have studied. On the contrary, formal business education is mostly focused on abilities that reinforce the left hemisphere of the brain. It should not surprise us, then, that most managers tend to avoid issues related to purpose, because they do not feel confident enough in this domain, and they fear they will look incompetent and lose credibility.

Since their default behavior is centered on rationality, argumentation, and persuasion, managers will look for ways of addressing purpose-related issues in these ways. In other words, they will avoid the adaptive challenge they face by resorting to technical remedies — a poor substitute for the adaptive work that is needed.

Here are some of the most typical technical remedies I've seen used to avoid the issue of purpose:

- Limiting the depth of work related to purpose to the definition and communication of the company's mission statement.
- Inspiring employees through a message that is inconsistent with top executives' behavior or the company's systems, processes, and practices.
- Confusing the narrative with a formal presentation that talks about facts, results, accomplishments, and new projects rather than history, stories, underlying values, and people.
- Trying to connect to people through formal activities in which top executives ask others to be open without opening up themselves; showing too much self-confidence and too little vulnerability.
- Looking at social responsibility as an obligation rather than as an opportunity for connecting to the community.

These technical remedies actually deflect attention from the adaptive work that needs to be done to make progress in the five variables related to purpose. Is there an antidote to the natural human tendency toward avoidance?

Yes, there is. Since purpose derives from the question of why we do what we do, a good antidote is simply to ask "Why?"

For example, imagine a meeting of your company's executive committee in which a new project is being discussed. If one of the members asked, "Why should we go ahead with the project?" the first answer would probably be along the lines of, "Because all the studies show that it will be profitable." But then the questioner could persist, asking, "But why this project and not another that is equally profitable?" Now the answer would probably be something like, "Because this is the one that makes the most sense given our strategy." This could lead to a third question like, "And why does that strategy make sense?" With each successive question, the group would be forced to get closer and closer to talking about the real purpose of the organization.

There are organizations, and individuals, that have a clear purpose and experience it vividly. In an organization of this kind, asking "Why?"

will rapidly connect to purpose, because members are used to relating everything they do to purpose. There are other organizations, and individuals, who do not have a clear purpose, and here the "Why?" question will have to be repeated many times, on all possible occasions, to force people to think about the purpose of what they are doing and thereby prevent avoidance.

An antidote, of course, is not a magical solution, but an effective reminder of the gap — between the aspiration of infusing an organization with purpose and the reality of not having it, in the case of this dimension — that is waiting to be more effectively addressed.

CHAPTER 5

STRATEGY: THE ORGANIZATION'S BRAIN

If people in your organization don't take reality into account, you have a problem. And that problem is likely connected to a lack of strategy.

The kind of large corporations we are so used to in our time were born with the Industrial Revolution. The key for their success was all about how they organized the work, meaning how they structured themselves to produce. The American mechanical engineer Frederick W. Taylor became the father of scientific management and the mentor of those who established and ran such companies, introducing the concept of efficiency. In 1906 he pronounced one of his famous lines: "In our scheme we do not ask for the initiative of our men. We do not want any initiative. All we want of them is to obey the orders we give them, do what we say, and do it quick."[42]

In this world, structure was far more important than strategy, not to mention abstract concepts like talent, culture or purpose. But things started changing over time, with a widely publicized step taken by General Motors in the 1920s, when they launched colored automobiles that made the classic black Ford's Model-T sales plummet. In the decades that followed, it would become clear that efficiency alone was not enough. The difference would have to do with adopting a distinct strategy, which in turn required an increasing number of people who would not simply obey but think. As it happens with the human body, having a fortified skeleton is important, but it is the brain that makes the difference and commands the skeleton.

HONDA AND AMAZON: STRATEGY AS A TOOL FOR ADAPTATION

In the fall of 1959, only four years after Honda had successfully launched production of motorcycles in Japan, a small group of Honda executives arrived in Los Angeles and rented an inexpensive apartment. It was the first step in Honda's attempt to bring its motorcycles to the United States, acting on founder Soichiro Honda's belief that the company's large 250cc and 305cc machines could be sold in America,

Honda knew the challenge would not be easy. The U.S. market was already occupied by dominant motorcycle brands, and expanding the number of potential customers would be difficult because motorcyclists had a bad image as black-leather jacket hoodlums. Making matters worse, Honda's initial sales efforts ran into an unexpected snag. The first Hondas sold in the United States quickly broke down, because Americans were accustomed to driving motorcycles longer and faster than the Japanese. Honda's reputation in the U.S. market took an immediate nosedive.

Near despair, Honda decided to change course. A few Honda executives in the United States had been driving tiny 50cc Supercub motorcycles from the company's American warehouse. A buyer from Sears had noticed these small vehicles and asked for permission to sell them to his customers. Although the Supercub was popular in Japan, Honda feared its diminutive size might negatively affect Honda's positioning in the macho U.S. market and rejected the Sears offer. Now, however, with the Honda brand seemingly on the verge of complete failure in the United States, Honda reversed course. The results were startling. Supported by a marketing campaign, sales of the Supercub rocketed, beginning Honda's transformation into the world's largest motorcycle manufacturer.[43]

If purpose is about *why*, strategy is about *what* (that is, vision and goals) and *how* (that is, means). Above all, strategy is thinking. It is using the brain to ask, "What do we want to attain?" and "How should we do it?" Strategic thinking means keeping this conversation alive, not once a year, but constantly.

When organizations limit their strategic thinking to an annual planning or budgeting process, strategy often becomes a straitjacket. Instead of rethinking the strategy when unexpected events occur, people focus on carrying out the actions planned using the resources allocated in the budget. This is a dangerous error, especially for organizations operating in unstable environments. For the same reason, it is a mistake to assume that formulating the strategy and implementing the strategy are two separate steps in a rigid sequence. Instead, these two activities must be continually intertwined. Implementation invariably generates a lot of information that should provide food for rethinking the strategy. Thus strategic thinking should be constant, not a once-a-year exercise.

When Soichiro Honda made the decision to launch his motorcycles in the American market, he knew little more than that there was an opportunity that should be pursued. He had a vague idea about the "what" and almost no idea about the "how." But he was conscious that more strategic thinking could come only from experimentation, not from sitting in a room and planning. And so he sent a bunch of executives with a limited budget to try out possible alternatives and learn.

Almost four decades later, another company applied similar strategic insight to a very different industry. In 1997, three years after the company's founding, Amazon issued its initial public stock offering, and thirty-three-year-old Jeff Bezos sent his first letter to the shareholders. The title was "It's all about the long term," reflecting the key idea behind Amazon's strategy: first become the number one player in the online retail market, then become profitable. In line with this strategy, Bezos asked those initial shareholders to be patient. "We will continue to make investment decisions in light of long-term market leadership considerations rather than short-term profitability considerations or short-term Wall Street reactions," he said in the letter, adding, "We will make bold rather than timid investment decisions where we see a sufficient probability of gaining market leadership advantages. Some of these investments will pay off, others will not, and we will have learned another valuable lesson in either case."[44]

Strategy cannot be a straitjacket, but neither can it be a loose sail in the wind. Strategy is not linear, nor is it solely instinct. Strategy demands experimentation, but experimentation that follows a certain path. Strategy requires both the ability to react in the short run and the willingness to persevere in the long run.

Jeff Bezos bet on the Internet and on the development of e-commerce. He understood something that was not obvious at the time: in the online world, there is space for only a few players in each industry. Based on that assumption, the "what" of Amazon's strategy had to be becoming the number one player in e-commerce, and the "how" had to be a tireless trial-and-error process involving continuous thinking and rethinking. This was the only way to innovate and respond to the challenges that would be posed by competitors, new technologies, changing customer preferences, and emerging regulations, among other unpredictable factors. This approach remains essential to Amazon's strategy, since in today's dynamic world achieving dominant scale, occupying an attractive niche, and exploiting unique resources are not enduring competitive advantages but must be achieved and re-achieved over and over as circumstances evolve.

It's a bit paradoxical: strategy is meant to provide stability by providing a set of guidelines that allow people to take certain things for granted. Yet our world pushes us toward instability, which means that strategy must be constantly re-evaluated and revised. The challenge, therefore, is understanding that a strategy's strength has less to do with providing clarity and lasting definitions, and more to do with its capacity to capture employees' initiative, to deal with unknowable events, and to redeploy resources as new opportunities emerge. In other words, instead of concentrating on becoming very good at doing any one particular thing, companies should concentrate on becoming very good at learning how to do new things — and the strategies they develop and follow must support and enhance that focus.

The more a strategy is designed to take into account new events that appear down the road and new initiatives that may be pushed by employees, the more adaptive the organization will be. At the same time, the degree to which a strategy must incorporate this element will depend on the kind of organization we are considering.

FIVE KEY VARIABLES: AWARENESS, REFLECTION, INVOLVEMENT, EXPERIMENTATION, SIMPLICITY

Within the dimension of strategy are five key variables you need to think about and measure in pursuing greater adaptive capacity:

1. *Awareness* of changing circumstances that may affect the organization
2. *Reflection* on these circumstances and on the response options available
3. *Involvement* of a broad range of your people in developing and testing strategy ideas

4. Continual *experimentation* with new strategic directions
5. *Simplicity*, which makes strategy easy to communicate, understand, and follow

Going back to Figure 1-1, you'll see these variables can increase your organization's adaptive capacity by strengthening the holding environment, enhancing the responsiveness, or both. Let's consider them one by one.

Awareness. When a doctor treats a patient, the first thing she will do is observe the symptoms (visible and invisible), conducting exams and gathering as much information as possible. Then she will interpret what is causing the symptoms and attempt to define the patient's illness. Only when she arrives at that definition will she prescribe treatment in an effort to alleviate the patient's symptoms.

The same process should be followed when authorities seek to improve the workings of a social system. Executives who head an organization have to continually observe the signals arriving from outside and inside the organization, interpret their significance and possible impact, and make decisions about how to intervene in the organization to mobilize it appropriately.

Back in 1994, the Cuetos observed that the airline industry was moving to an open-sky policy and that most potential competitors in Latin America were still state-owned companies. Under these circumstances, they thought they had an opportunity if they bought LAN Airlines. In similar fashion, Jeff Bezos, observing the development of the Internet, understood that a whole new market was about to emerge and that he had an opportunity if he could move fast to seize it. In the same way, Soichiro Honda realized that he had an opportunity to conquer America with his motorcycles at a time when Japanese automotive companies had not yet looked across the Pacific Ocean.

A good strategy starts from being aware of what is going on — in society, in politics, in the economy, in the industry, with competitors, with suppliers, with clients, within the company — indeed, everywhere. Being constantly aware of what is happening allows top executives to help people in the organization understand the evolving reality, to think about the future, and to anticipate the emergence of opportunities. Without this awareness, quick response to rapid change will be impossible.

Having as many people as possible aware of changing circumstances will surely increase the organization's adaptive capacity by enhancing its responsiveness — because awareness is a key variable affecting adaptive capacity.

When thinking about your own organization, ask yourself, "Does the top team meet regularly to talk about what is happening inside and outside our organization?" and "Does the top team continually gather and convey information from and to people in the company?"

Reflection. Observation is not enough. Interpretation is where the real thinking takes place, and it is also where the practice of reflection comes into the game. Without reflection, choosing among complex options — a crucial element of strategy — is practically impossible.

Bezos, like many other businesspeople, was aware of the opportunity that the Internet opened, but understanding how to take advantage of it was another matter. Meeting with his team to reflect on the steps they were taking and the meaning of the events they observed around them was key in Amazon's success. In fact, it was that reflective process that led them to challenge the widespread assumption that profit was more important than market share.

Challenging assumptions, both those held in the industry and those held within the company, is a crucial aspect of the reflection process. Bill Gates himself had bet against the Internet when shaping Microsoft's strategy for the mid-'90s, but his top team was later able to challenge that flawed assumption, consequently changing their strategy.

Business decision makers have one advantage that physicians lack: they can use intervention as part of the interpretative process. In other words, they can run experiments to test their interpretation of events, collect new information, and engage in further reflection — all leading to new and better decisions and more effective interventions. Such experimentation is extremely helpful in making the strategy realistic, since strategizing must take into account not just future possibilities but also present restraints, including gaps in the company's capabilities that need to be identified and overcome.

Like awareness, reflection will also increase the organization's adaptive capacity by enhancing its responsiveness, because the process of reflection forces managers to make sense of what is going on.

When thinking about your own organization, ask yourself, "Is it normal practice for our top team members to come up with different plausible interpretations about the realities we face, and for these interpretations to be openly discussed and analyzed?" and "Are people in our top team authorized by the group to play the role of devil's advocate, allowing unpopular interpretations to be presented and debated?"

Involvement. Strategy is about thinking, and in the organizational context thinking is typically left to top executives. The rest are in charge of implementing what has been thought and decided — the strategy. Unfortunately, this traditional way of seeing the organization makes it less adaptive than otherwise, incapable of taking full advantage of its members' potential.

The opposite alternative might be to have everyone participate in developing the strategy, which seems unrealistic. How can people, then, contribute with their ideas and experience to the strategy? The answer lies in distinguishing the *what* and the *how* of the strategy, as well as in removing the traditional barrier between the development and implementation stages of the strategy.

Task Force Tarawa's mission — the *what* within Operation Iraqi Freedom — was securing the eastern part of Nasiriyah. Top officials developed a plan to accomplish that goal — the *how*. However, the plan could not be implemented as initially conceived, which meant revising it almost every night, using the information and insights provided by the actual soldiers who were fighting in the field. (This is normal in the military context. Part of the Marines' culture is the understanding that "No plan survives first contact," meaning that reality will always differ from what was assumed in the plan.) For Task Force Tarawa, the *what* did not change and they had no input on it, but the *how* was constantly changing, and they did have an input there; they understood that their job included developing this aspect of the strategy as well as implementing it.

The more adaptive the strategy's content is, the more involvement it will require from people, especially in the *how*, which will be built in a back-and-forth process between elaboration and implementation. Lou Gerstner understood from the beginning that this was the case with IBM. By contrast, General Motors executives never understood that they needed to involve Saab executives and engineers in thinking about the future of the Swedish company.

Involving people in developing and testing strategy ideas will increase an organization's adaptive capacity by both strengthening the holding environment and enhancing its responsiveness. This is because people become more engaged when they feel their opinions are taken into account (which strengthens the holding capacity), and because having more people engaged in the *what* and in the *how* process provides more information and insights (which enhances responsiveness).

When thinking about your own organization, ask yourself, "Are our people asked to consider how they will implement the company's strategic definitions in their own area of concern?" and "Is our top team accustomed to rethinking certain aspects of the strategy based on the experience reported by those who are implementing it?"

Experimentation. As we saw in Chapter 3, evolution is not about big changes but rather about small changes that will make a difference. Those changes take place through an experimentation process that calls for testing variations, many of which fail, making selections from among the variations that succeed, and looking for amplification of those selections. Thus adaptation does not happen without experimentation.

This means that an essential part of strategic thinking must be running as many experiments as possible. This certainly demands a risk-taking attitude, but it should be a smart one. It is not about running experiments that will put the whole company at risk or that contradict what is essential to it. It is about running experiments that will let people learn and thrive by testing new approaches to products, services, business models, systems, processes, or practices.

Sending a small group of executives to Los Angeles with a limited budget to test the American motorcycle market was an experiment that Soichiro Honda decided to run. The initial experiment was a failure, but those executives then ran another experiment by making the small 50cc Supercubs available for sale in a market where large motorcycles had previously dominated. This second experiment worked.

Not all experiments have to be initiated from the top down. The strategy can be designed to allow employees at all levels to propose and run experiments. Those that succeed may be scaled up to become part of the company's core strategy. This is what happens when a company allows its people to spend 20 percent of their time thinking about and working on whatever creation or improvement they come up with, as Google does. The results so far include Google Desktop, Google Docs, Google Maps, Google Mail, and Google News, just to name a few.

Experimentation increases an organization's adaptive capacity by enhancing its responsiveness, because experiments force you to continuously look at reality to test new options. But it also helps to strengthen the holding environment when the experiments are run in a bottom-up fashion, allowing employees at all levels to have an impact on the company's progress.

When thinking about your own organization, ask yourself, "How does our strategy provide space for experimentation?" and "How many of our people feel authorized to experiment, and how many experiments are being run?"

Simplicity. Traditional business strategies — three- to five-year plans full of detailed actions to be implemented — no longer fit in the current world. They were meant for the last decades of the industrial era, when companies felt the need for precise definitions in an environment that had already begun to be less clear and predictable. Even then, such detailed and rigid strategies were largely ineffective. Today, the current levels of uncertainty most companies face make such attempts useless. This was confirmed as long ago as 1993 by Jack Welch, the CEO of the company considered the founder of strategic planning: "Trying to define what will happen three to five years out, in specific, quantitative terms, is a futile exercise."[45]

Nowadays, strategy is less like a realistic painting than an impressionistic one. In the former, everything is perfectly outlined, leaving no space for improvisation or additions. In the latter, there is a powerful idea, imperfectly outlined, that invites more brushes to come in, adding detail, color, and form. At some of the most adaptive companies, the strategy may even look like a blank canvas, ready to be painted, even its shape and size subject to change.

In this new environment, good strategies are simple, easy to convey, and easier to understand. The *what* and the *how* become clear and appealing to all those who work for the company. Even though the environment may be complex, a good strategy will respond to that complexity with a single organizing idea that will easily fit within the company's narrative and thus be clearly connected to its purpose.

One example of this was Walgreens during the 1980s, which made a strategic decision about moving from being a drugstore to becoming a convenience drugstore. Following this simple idea, internal efforts fell naturally into place, looking for the best locations, offering more products, clustering many stores within a small radius, pioneering drive-through pharmacies, investing in technology, and shifting the financial focus from profit per store to profit per customer visit. The Walgreens strategy worked because it was easy to convey, easy to understand, and a good starting point for aligning a host of specific decisions and activities.[46]

Because simplicity makes the strategy easy to communicate, understand, and follow, it increases the organization's adaptive capacity by strengthening its holding environment. When people are able to connect what they do to a broader context, they feel more fully a part of that context.

When thinking about your own organization, ask yourself, "Can you describe your company's strategy to the person standing next to you in the elevator before he gets off?" and "Is the main concept in our strategy appealing enough for employees to want to make the strategy their own?"

STRATEGY IN VARIOUS KINDS OF ORGANIZATIONS

Regardless of their nature, all organizations need a strategy. This is as valid for a government as for a school, for an IT company as for a manufacturer, for a church as for an NGO. It is even valid for a family and an individual. Thinking about what we want to attain and how we are going to attain it is always necessary, especially when the reality we live in continually increases in complexity.

However, a strategy may take different forms, some of which help the organization become more adaptive, while others do not. An innovative company like Amazon should have a very simple strategy based on a handful of powerful concepts, with no further detail. This is because its environment changes quickly, constantly giving rise to unpredictable opportunities and threats. A detailed strategic plan with the *how* expressed in concrete steps and actions might cause those opportunities and threats to be missed. Amazon needs a strategy in which the *how* is expressed only in broad definitions.

By contrast, Honda is an action-driven kind of organization whose production timelines are longer, making it inherently difficult for Honda to adapt to changes immediately. Honda can work with a strategic plan, setting goals, objectives, and actions in different layers. But the plan must have open spaces in which to experiment and let new ideas and opportunities emerge. Otherwise the company might lose connection with the way its environment is evolving and may fail to adapt in response.

To see how much progress your company could attain in coming up with a strategy that makes it a more adaptive organization, go back to Figure 2-2 and use the kind of organization your industry is closest to as a benchmark. Generally speaking, we should expect communal and innovative organizations to have strategies that define only broad concepts, leaving space for people's ideas and initiatives, since these organizations do more adaptive than technical work and therefore are more participatory and less hierarchical. Bureaucratic and action-driven organizations, on the other hand, should be expected to have strategic plans with clearer and more detailed definitions, since they do more technical than adaptive work and therefore are more hierarchical and less participatory.

To get even more specific, let's look in Figure 5-1 at the five variables related to the strategy dimension and see how they should look for each kind of organization, resorting again to the music equalizer metaphor.

Figure 5-1. The strategy equalizer

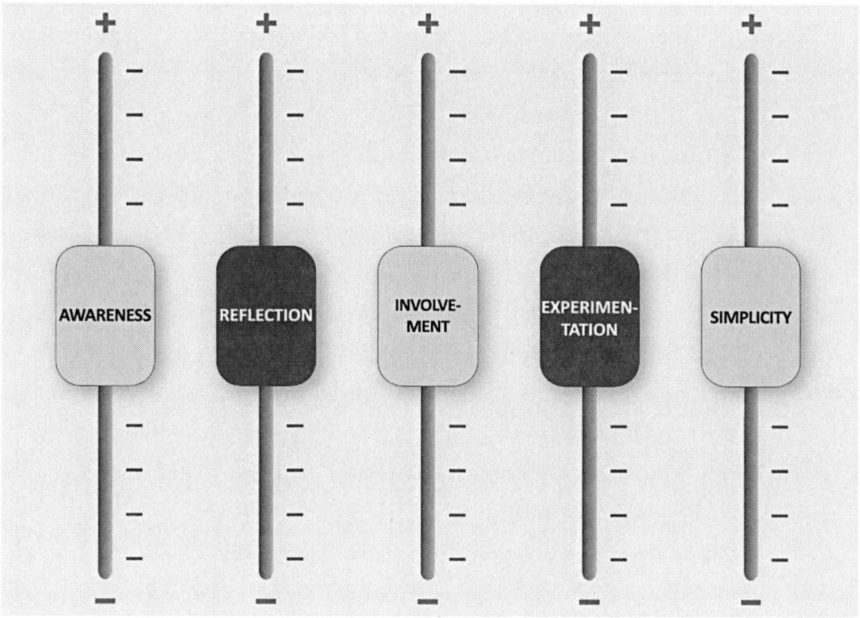

When thinking about an innovative organization, all five knobs in the strategy equalizer should be turned toward the upper range, as high as possible. The type of work these companies do is highly adaptive, which demands a lot of reflection, involvement, and emergent experimentation. At the same time, these companies exist in a very unstable environment, which calls for permanent awareness, simple and powerful concepts that serve as guides to action, and rapid experimentation. Amazon illustrates the effectiveness of this kind of strategic thinking for an innovative organization.

In the case of a communal organization, since the environment is more stable, rapid reaction time is less of a critical factor than it is for an innovative organization. Because the external pressures are not high and more time is available, awareness will typically be in the middle range. Given that the organization is internally focused, there is more room for conversations and clarifications, which means that simplicity can also be set at the mid-range. On the other hand, reflection and involvement will be in the upper range, higher than experimentation. Even though these organizations should be good at experimenting because they are participatory by nature, a stable environment will lessen the need for it. (If we apply these observations to political parties, which are communal kind of organizations, we can begin to understand why it is hard for them to change, despite the demands for change they may receive from citizens.)

Action-driven organizations are forced to be good at experimentation by the unstable environments to which they are exposed. However, experiments will usually be centrally planned rather than being left to employees' initiative. Thus, the experimentation knob should typically be in the mid-range, with fewer experiments than in an innovative organization, though with experiments that are usually better designed and financially supported. Because action-driven organizations are externally oriented, awareness should be in the upper range. The same applies to simplicity, because the work tends to be more technical. But because of time constraints, these two variables often become neglected. Reflection and involvement will usually appear in the lower range; these constitute the big challenge to be faced when a company starts moving upward in Figure 2-2, adding more complexity to the work it performs, as Telefonica did.

Lastly, a bureaucratic organization will have all five knobs in the lower range. It's possible that the organization may have the capacity and resources to work on all of these variables, but it does not need to do so. Which incentives does a utility company have to devote time and effort to these variables when it faces little competition and the work it performs is routinary? The only possible exception is awareness, which may need to be somewhat higher because of today's increasingly empowered citizens and consumers.

HOW COMPANIES AVOID STRATEGIC THINKING, AND THE POWER OF ASKING "WHY NOT?"

In biological terms, the major difference between humans and all other species is the extent to which the brain has developed. Despite the enormous adaptive advantage this factor provides, many organizations and societies still live in Henry Ford's paradigm, wondering, "Why is it that whenever I ask for a pair of hands, a brain comes attached?"

Today, however, the traditional assumption that an organization should have only a few people who think and a large number who execute is badly outdated. Jack Welch challenged it in the '80s by empowering people; Jeff Bezos went a step further in the '90s by encouraging people to take risks; and in the '00s, Sergey Brin and Larry Page decided to create an organization that, from its very inception, positioned people's initiative and creativity as its main assets, to be managed accordingly. Google's success testifies to their foresightedness.

Despite the growing acceptance of this new reality, too many organizations still behave as if the leap to action is the default setting: instead of thinking and then acting, they skip the former and focus on the latter. The subprime crisis in the late '00s was caused by this pattern of behavior. The signals that something was wrong in the banking system were flashing everywhere, but most bankers were too immersed in trying to take advantage of the bubble to pause, reflect, and realize that following the market made no sense. The few who raised their voices were silenced or ignored because it was easier to continue acting than to stop and think.

Why do so many people in organizations fall into this trap, avoiding the thinking that would take them out of their comfort zone to discover new possibilities? In most cases, the reason is the fear of losing traction, especially when businesses are working well. As the saying goes, "There is nothing harder than to stop doing what we do well." Or, we might add, "what we think we are doing well."

The default behavior of leaping to action gets expressed through various specific avoidance mechanisms that lead people to treat strategy as technical rather than adaptive work. Here are some of the most typical avoidance mechanisms:

- Confusing strategizing with budgeting, which means limiting strategic thinking to an annual discussion of the percentage by which the financial goals should be increased.
- Confusing strategic thinking with strategic planning, which moves people to immediately engage in developing an action plan, skipping the tougher and more productive questions associated with what we want to become and how we should get there.
- Bringing in guest speakers to lecture executives about current trends and issues of relevance to the business without subsequent internal debriefings that could make practical use of the insights gained.
- Resorting to various mechanisms for asking employees for new ideas about improving the business without providing support for the implementation of those that are approved and feedback about those that are discarded.
- Opening opportunities for experimentation only when they pose little or no risk.

These technical ways of facing strategy avoid the essential ingredient — thinking — and divert attention from the adaptive work that needs to be done to make progress in the five crucial variables, which creates the illusion that everything is fine in this dimension of strategy.

Is there an antidote for this problem? Yes. It consists of asking, "Why not?" If the question "Why?" points toward the ultimate reason for what we do, the question "Why not?" leads us to challenge conventional wisdom and find reasons for what we hesitate to do.

For example, imagine a sales meeting in which a new executive proposes an untested idea for increasing the department's performance. Two older executives immediately reject the idea, declaring flatly, "It will never work here." If there is no one empowered to ask "Why not?" it is likely there will be no further discussion. But if the question is asked and a real answer is required, the group will be forced to think, to involve more people in the conversation, and perhaps decide that running an experiment to test the new idea might be worthwhile. If the experiment succeeds, the idea could be scaled up and, perhaps, become part of the core strategy.

In other cases, asking "Why not stop doing this?" may be an important question to ask when a cherished project or department has stopped performing well and, according to a seriously done reality test, should be closed.

Whatever the final decision may be in any specific case, asking "Why not?" forces a company to be more aware of what is going on, to reflect, to involve more employees in various aspects of the strategy, to experiment with new ideas, and to arrive at simple strategic concepts that most people can understand and support.

CHAPTER 6

STRUCTURE: THE ORGANIZATION'S SKELETON

If people in your organization are not reaching their potential because they feel constrained by the excess of rigidity and control, you have a problem. And that problem is likely connected to structure.

The skeleton in a human body is not just a collection of bones but an integrated whole connected through several articulations and a nervous system that transmits neural signals between the brain and the rest of the body, which provides the necessary coordination among all parts. Interestingly, the nervous system includes neural circuits that can independently control reflexes and central pattern generators without having to go back to the brain, which allows for faster responses. This, too, has its parallel in the workings of an organization.

All organizations need a structure, just as the human body needs a skeleton. In both cases, the challenge is to have the necessary degree of control with as little rigidity as possible, a combination that maximizes the organism's adaptive capacity. Though the skeleton of a weightlifter will be more rigid than the skeleton of a gymnast, both would benefit from lowering that rigidity, but not to the point where their activities are hampered (there is a good reason why a weightlifter wears a support belt). Similarly, despite the different kinds of organizations that exist, all of them would benefit from lowering rigidity as far as possible without hampering their unique pattern of activities.

3M, MCDONALD'S, AND THE U.S. MARINES: DIFFERENT STRUCTURES FOR DIFFERENT ADAPTIVE CHALLENGES

3M is considered one of the most innovative organizations in the world. Its company folklore includes the tale of a reporter who kept asking, without success, for a copy of 3M's organizational chart. Finally the company president admitted, "We have one of those charts, but we don't like to wave it around. There are some great people who might get upset if they found out who their bosses are."[47]

The story may be apocryphal, but it reflects the truth that an organizational chart can never reflect the depth of the coordination mechanisms that every company requires. 3M understands this and therefore does not fall into the trap of limiting its coordination mechanisms to fancy titles and job descriptions captured on a chart. To do so would certainly damage the company's adaptive capacity.

This doesn't mean, of course, that organizational charts are worthless, but you have to be aware about their limitations, on one hand, and the fact that some of them imply more structural rigidity and control than others, on the other. A matrix design, for example, is less rigid and control-oriented than a multi-divisional design, and a multi-divisional design in turn is less rigid and control-oriented than a functional design. Although not all organizations should have a matrix design, all should aspire to have the least rigid and control-oriented structure possible, since an excess of rigidity and control limit the expression of people's potential.

McDonald's finally came to this realization shortly before the turn of the twenty-first century. One of the key management features of the company had been its standardized products and service, providing the same experience in whichever of the thousands of restaurants in over a hundred countries you chose to visit. But McDonald's eventually realized that owing to local competition and changes in nutritional habits, some degree of flexibility had to be allowed within that standardization. This was made possible by regional decentralization in the decision-making process, with no need of relevant changes in the organizational chart. Of course, the Big Mac is still exactly the same all over the world, but from one country to the next there are some variations in the menu. What's more, within a global framework of common goals, policies, and guidelines provided at the corporate level, individual geographic business units have the freedom to develop programs and performance measures appropriate to local conditions.

Even less rigidity and control are ingrained in the structure of the U.S. Marine Corps, despite an organizational chart that includes ten ranks of officers and nine ranks of enlisted personnel. As a retired lieutenant who fought in Iraq said to me:

> We are told from the very beginning that decentralized control and junior officer initiative is key to success in battle. We are taught, as leaders, to always give specific objectives and what we call "left and right lateral limits" within which we want our subordinates to operate. Within these very broad boundaries, we want our juniors to literally run wild, with us pulling back on the leash when necessary. We believe in supervision, but never micro-management. We want solutions, not questions. I want all of my Marines to be independently thinking and making decisions based on their knowledge of the objectives of our unit two levels above them. I cannot emphasize enough how this shapes our character.[48]

When an order is given, it is mandatory to state what is called the "commander's intent," which provides the link between the mission and the execution as well as basis for subordinates to exercise initiative when unanticipated opportunities arise or when the original plan no longer applies. This intent is normally captured in a statement that is four or five sentences long, and must be understood two echelons down. The result? A hierarchical but flexible structure that provides high levels of adaptive capacity to the organization.

Finding the right structural balance between freedom and rigidity is an eternal dilemma; there are advantages and disadvantages on both sides. Differentiating among the four kinds of organizations will help us in figuring out where the correct balance should be. But it is also important to distinguish between functions that need more freedom and those that need more rigidity and control. Sales and product development are among the former, whereas accounting and legal issues are among the latter. In other words, the presence of more adaptive work calls for more freedom, and the presence of more technical work calls for more rigidity and control.

Most important, the structure must be tailored to the needs of the organization, based upon its industry, its stage of development, the external realities it faces, the strategy it employs, and especially its people and culture. Indeed, in unstable environments the classic idea that structure follows strategy is unrealistic, because the strategy largely emerges from the organization itself and its execution depends on that same organization, not the organization that may exist five or ten years in the future.

It is also unrealistic to think that a structure — including the organizational chart, the role definitions, the decision-making process, and other processes and systems — will be able to embody and shape all the coordination needs and relationships within a company. In the end, the organization's purpose and culture also play key roles in aligning people. The purpose serves as the glue that keeps people together, and the culture serves as the oil that makes the coordination system work. Structure matters, yes — but only as one crucial element in a larger, highly complex, organic system.

FIVE KEY VARIABLES: DECENTRALIZATION, FLEXIBILITY, STEERING/STIRRING COMMITTEES, INTRAPRENEURSHIP, EXTERNAL NETWORKS

Within the dimension of structure are five key variables you need to think about and measure in pursuing greater adaptive capacity:

1. *Decentralization* of decision making
2. *Flexibility* in procedures and activities
3. The use of *steering/stirring committees* to engage people in adaptive work
4. The encouragement of *intrapreneurship*
5. The use of *external networks* rather than relying only on internal sources

If we go back to Figure 1-1, these variables can increase your organization's adaptive capacity by strengthening the holding environment, enhancing the responsiveness, or both. Let's consider them one by one.

Decentralization. The most typical way of controlling an organization is by centralizing decisions, making sure that everything that matters is resolved at the higher levels. This reduces employees' freedom and autonomy as well as the adaptive capacity of the organization. Everything becomes slower, because issues get stuck in the top executives' hands. At the same time, the company misses the opportunity of providing its employees with learning experiences that will allow them to be better decision makers, allowing the organization to be more sustainable and less dependent on the talents of a few individuals.

The U.S. Marine Corps is a hierarchical organization, yet it tries to be as decentralized as possible because making quick decisions is a critical advantage in combat. The same is true for all companies that live in unstable environments, no matter how hierarchical they are.

However, decentralized decision making requires that people have information and understand the boundaries of the terrain in which they are playing. Like members of the Marines, they need to know the general criteria, set one or two levels higher, that should guide their decisions. It's easy to recognize an organization that is run on this basis. For example, a Starbucks customer can recognize that the coffee chain is relatively decentralized by the fact that an individual barista is permitted to replace a customer's bad-tasting cup of coffee for free without asking a supervisor for permission.

A way to force a degree of decentralization is by expanding bosses' span of control. As the number of direct reports increases, a manager's capacity to control them will decrease, forcing him to give those reports more freedom, thereby flattening the organization. This is the case at Google, for example, where managers have 30 reports on average. A similar effect occurs when a company like 3M encourages the creation of business units, each managed like an individual company.

Decentralized decision making increases an organization's adaptive capacity mainly by enhancing its responsiveness, because people are encouraged to make quick decisions based on the information they have rather than scale up issues and involve bosses on top.

When thinking about your own organization, ask yourself, "Are employees encouraged to make independent decisions and provided with sufficient information to do so?" and "Do bosses resist the temptation to make decisions that could be made by their subordinates, even when they are asked to make them?"

Flexibility. The most typical sources of rigidity in an organization are standard procedures that govern operations and activities, as well as formalities like job types of descriptions, behavioral rules, written communications, and dress codes. Both types of mechanisms reduce the organization's flexibility and, ultimately, its adaptive capacity.

In many cases, standardization and formalization may help an organization move faster by predefining the way people have to act in particular circumstances. These constitute a form of decentralization, empowering people lower in the organization to make certain very well specified decisions. This is the way bureaucracies operate. The problem arises when the circumstances differ from those defined in the protocols — that is, when reality changes. In these cases, technical work gives way to adaptive work, standardization and formalization fail, and the organization with little or no flexibility is ill prepared to cope.

This is why, as the varying circumstances McDonald's faced in different regions of the world continued to multiply, the company decided to reduce the density of its manuals and procedures, opening more space for customization. The same learning has taken place in many other multinational companies that initially tried to standardize everything, only to discover that reality is too variable to fit a handful of rigid, inflexible structures.

On the other hand, this does not mean that you want to have complete flexibility and that nothing should be standardized or formalized. The distinction between technical and adaptive work must be the key criterion, and system-shaping tools such as enterprise resource planning (ERP) software should factor this in so as to avoid becoming straitjackets that hamper necessary freedom of action.

More flexibility increases an organization's adaptive capacity by enhancing its responsiveness, because people in a flexible organization are less tied to standardizations and formalities that limit their potential to see and act beyond their defined areas of control. Nonetheless, boundaries provided by structure can help to strengthen the holding environment, thereby also increasing adaptive capacity. Thus, even the most innovative organizations need certain rules (such as timelines) to foster creativity, which means that the highest adaptive capacity is not attained through unlimited flexibility.[49]

When thinking about your own organization, ask yourself, "What are the assumptions behind our standardization and formalization of procedures and activities?" and "Do employees feel authorized to introduce more flexibility to procedures and forms when they prevent the organization from responding effectively to the demands it faces?"

Steering/stirring committees. Companies and their employees tend to dislike meetings; many people assume that they are a waste of time. This may or not be true, depending on the purpose and the dynamic of the meeting. This is another case in which drawing the distinction between technical and adaptive work is helpful.

Meetings that are focused on technical issues should be limited in number and length. Such meetings normally involve distributing information, checking a list of activities, or improving some minor coordination issues. When these meetings are necessary, they should be short and straightforward.

The real challenge is meetings that touch on adaptive issues, because they demand conversation and learning. This means hearing different perspectives, understanding, engaging, and aligning. Everything is messier and the results are not always clear, often demanding further conversation. People tend to feel uncomfortable with meetings of this kind, which are not at all short and straightforward.

This leads to a paradoxical result: organizations typically devote more time to gathering people to discuss technical work than adaptive work, when it should be exactly the other way around. Important issues related to adaptive work don't get discussed, and problems therefore go unresolved.

3M has learned to avoid this dilemma. People engage in conversations because they understand that it is precisely the exchange of ideas, perspectives, and positions that allows them to thrive. And here is where committees become relevant, especially those that bring together people from different departments, units, or divisions, and sometimes external stakeholders as well. For example, when 3M's Post-it Note team wanted to accelerate product development, it had the team's marketing, financial, and other nonmembers move into the same building with the technology developers. We call these *steering/stirring committees* because they help not only to manage linear processes but also to "stir the pot" of the organization so that tough issues and differences are not avoided but addressed.

These steering/stirring committees increase an organization's adaptive capacity by both strengthening the holding environment and enhancing its responsiveness. The committees' "steering" role strengthens the holding environment by connecting people despite their differences, and their "stirring" role increases flexibility by ensuring that differences emerge and are considered.

When thinking about your own organization, ask yourself, "Do our people differentiate meetings for technical work and meetings for adaptive work?" and "Does our structure contemplate and value the existence of permanent and temporary committees that bring together different stakeholders from throughout the organization?"

Intrapreneurship. People who are smart and have initiative need space to grow their ideas. They can do it as entrepreneurs, on their own or with some friends, or as intrapreneurs within an established company. There is a tradeoff between these two alternatives, the first providing more autonomy and the second more resources. This tradeoff, in turn, creates a dilemma for organizations: if they wish to attract and retain potential intrapreneurs, they have to grant them not just resources but also autonomy, which implies a low level of control but also the danger of silos that may risk the company's unity and identity.

Devising the right formula for intrapreneurship has proven to be tricky. Monetary incentives will help you retain the most talented self-starters, but even more important is feeding their sense of shared purpose (the glue that keeps people together) and reinforcing their connection to the organizational culture (the oil that makes the coordination system flow). Many companies have tried to capture the spirit of intrapreneurship and failed. I have witnessed many cases, in different industries, in which intrapreneurs were turned down by authorities and their projects ended up dying.

3M managed to find a way to provide its intrapreneurs with the freedom they need without sacrificing the company's unity. As William McKnight, the legendary executive who headed the company for four decades, put it back in 1948: "As our business grows, it becomes increasingly necessary to delegate responsibility and to encourage men and women to exercise their initiative. This requires considerable tolerance. Those men and women to whom we delegate authority and responsibility, if they are good people, are going to want to do their jobs in their own way."[50]

Creating a structure flexible enough to allow these intrapreneurs to grow and operate across boundaries can greatly increase an organization's adaptive capacity. The resulting structure resembles a spiderweb — a network of people who interact with one another, forming self-organized cross-functional teams, performing specific functions but also taking the initiative to improve products and services and create new ones, always in collaboration with others. This is what happens at 3M, where a project team can evolve into a division, as well as at Google, but it also happens to a lesser extent in hierarchical companies like LAN Airlines, where the service standard was defined by a team of flight attendants, and Volvo, where automobiles are assembled from start to finish by teams of self-managing workers at the Kalmar Plant in Sweden.[51]

Encouraging intrapreneurship increases the organization's adaptive capacity by enhancing its responsiveness, since it means there will be more people willing to develop fresh ideas and initiatives quickly and effectively.

When thinking about your own organization, ask yourself, "How does our structure grant space for people's initiative?" and "What kind of work is done to keep people connected to our company's identity without killing their autonomy?"

External networks. The following paragraph is part of an internal memo that Stephen Elop sent to his staff in February 2011, four months after being appointed as the first foreign CEO in the history of Nokia, the Finnish cell phone company:

> The battle of devices has now become a war of ecosystems, where ecosystems include not only the hardware and software of the device, but developers, applications, ecommerce, advertising, search, social applications, location-based services, unified communications and many other things. Our competitors aren't taking our market share with devices; they are taking our market share with an entire ecosystem.[52]

Nokia was facing a serious adaptive challenge. After fifteen years as the world leader in sales of mobile devices, Nokia had been losing market share ever since the introduction of smartphones. (A year later, it would hand over its number one position to Samsung.) The problem, as Elop explained, was Nokia's failure to create an ecosystem comparable to the ones surrounding its competitors. For example, Apple's iOS and Google's Android operating systems for smartphones both capitalized on broad networks of hardware and software partners that enormously enhanced the value provided to smartphone customers.

Elop concluded that Nokia needed an ecosystem of its own. A couple of months later, he forged an alliance with his former employer, Microsoft, which made possible the development of Nokia's Lumia smartphones, run with the Windows Phone operating system. Based on the success of this alliance, Microsoft decided two years later to acquire Nokia's mobile phone business, bringing back Elop as the new head of the Devices Division.

The smartphone market isn't the only one in which collaboration is now crucial to business success. In one industry after another, concepts like ecosystem and inclusive business are being discussed more and more. The idea of having everything designed and produced within a single company is now almost obsolete; alliances and networks are now just as important externally as they are internally. And the underlying principle is the same: in a complex world, know-how is widely distributed, and only a flexible structure makes it possible to bring together enough of that know-how to make the organization sufficiently adaptive.

External networks are a highly effective way of increasing an organization's adaptive capacity by enhancing its responsiveness. These partnerships are like the tentacles that keep a company connected to the external world.

When thinking about your own organization, ask yourself, "How inclined are our top executives to build external alliances as opposed to trying to do everything internally?" and "Is our structure permeable enough to support those alliances?"

STRUCTURE IN VARIOUS KINDS OF ORGANIZATIONS

As we've seen, every organizational structure should be tailored to the specific needs of the organization it serves. But whatever form the structure takes, it's important for that structure to enhance rather than limit the organization's adaptive capacity.

To see how much progress your company could attain in coming up with a structure that makes it a more adaptive organization, go back to Figure 2-2 and use the kind of organization your industry is closest to as a benchmark. Generally speaking, we expect communal and innovative organizations to have structures that grant more freedom and impose less rigidity and control, providing space for people's ideas and initiatives, since they do more adaptive than technical work and therefore are more participatory and less hierarchical. By contrast, bureaucratic organizations should be expected to have high degrees of rigidity and control and almost no freedom, since discretionary decision making is not desirable and most of the work is technical. The action-driven organization is a special case — despite its hierarchical nature, which encourages stricter control, it has to move quickly given the unstable environment it lives in. The result is a permanent tension between control and freedom.

To be more specific, take a look at the five variables related to the structure dimension and see how they would look like for each kind of organization. This should serve as a benchmark for your own company, depending on the kind of organization it is closest to. Figure 6-1 depicts these variables as the knobs of an equalizer, which you'd have to move in order to make your organization become more adaptive.

Figure 6-1. The structure equalizer

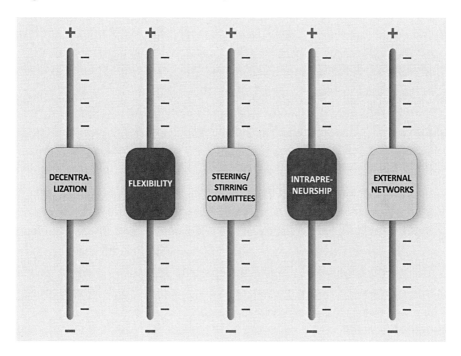

The structure of an innovative organization must be the least rigid and control-oriented in order to grant people the necessary freedom to unleash all their creativity and initiative. Rigidity and control tend to limit that potential and create distrust, which may drive creative people to leave. Therefore, all the knobs in the structure equalizer should be turned to the upper range, with the caveat that the flexibility knob *should not* be turned to the very top of the range, since, as mentioned above, a minimum number of rules are needed to hold people together, even in an innovative organization.

In a communal organization, the structure knobs' adjustment will be similar to those of an innovative organization, except for steering/stirring committees, which will be in the mid-range, and intrapreneurship, which will be in the lower range. Because this is an internally oriented organization, the sense of community and the importance of identity will take precedence over the need for autonomy. In other words, the group will see people with too much self-initiative as a threat to the status quo and to the intrinsic sense of equality that should prevail.

For a different reason, the lack of autonomy will also be a characteristic of a bureaucratic organization, in which no individual initiative is allowed. On the contrary, standardization and formalization are the norm, and the flexibility knob will therefore be in the lower range. This in turn explains why decentralized decision making will rank high, because everything is predefined and people at lower levels simply apply the prescribed norms to any decision with no discretion at all. External networks will not be relevant, because autarky is the norm, and stirring committees will also be in the lower range. Where committees exist, they will tend to waste time on technical issues, and no disequilibrium will be generated in regard to adaptive issues.

Finally, an action-driven organization will exist in a permanent state of tension. Its nature pushes toward more control, which means bringing the knobs down. But the instability of the environment and the need to react as fast as possible to the changes taking place will push for more freedom and less control, moving the knobs upward. Typically, an action-driven organization will have knobs in the mid-range of the equalizer, mirroring the permanent struggle between its internal nature and the external reality it inhabits.

HOW COMPANIES AVOID RETHINKING THEIR STRUCTURE, AND THE POWER OF ASKING "WHAT WOULD YOU DO?"

Environmental changes during recent decades have produced enormous evolutionary pressures on organizational structures. The size of many companies has dramatically increased; many have expanded into different countries and continents; new information technologies have transformed communication systems; employees are better educated and eager for more autonomy; products and services have become more sophisticated, and so on. Structures need to change to cope with these changes, and in fact a lot of adaptive work has been done in this regard.

We've seen how McDonald's finally changed its structure, making it more flexible by reducing the degree of standardization; how the U.S. Marines introduced more autonomy into the decision-making processes of its soldiers in combat; and how companies like 3M have resisted formalization in favor of flexibility.

Of course, not all organizations should aim to have flexible structures. But all organizations should seek to reduce their level of rigidity and control to the lowest level they can attain without losing effectiveness in their business. Fortunately, a stronger purpose and a stronger culture allow for a less rigid structure, because when people act under common values and norms — the essence of culture, as we shall see — the resulting social control is able to replace the formal control provided by structure, at least in part.[53]

Nevertheless, the default behavior of too many managers in too many industries is still to exercise control over people rather than granting them freedom. They assume that effectiveness comes from getting things under control, and hence they have a reasonable fear of losing effectiveness if that control is given away. Their tendency to revert to the command-and-control default setting counteracts efforts to raise the knobs of the structure dimension as a way of avoiding the adaptive challenge. Some of the most typical avoidance mechanisms in the area of structure include:

- Changing the structural design — for example, to a matrix design — without addressing the changes in loyalties, attitudes, and behaviors that will have to accompany the change to make it work.

- Signing agreements with external stakeholders, like suppliers, without building the kind of trust relationship needed to create a real alliance for collaboration and innovation, the basis of an ecosystem.
- Trying to decentralize by delegating tasks without giving up any real decision-making power.
- Trying to decentralize by delegating tasks and decision-making power without providing opportunities for guidance and feedback.
- Creating initiatives aimed at promoting intrapreneurship — internal contests, for example — without allocating the necessary material and human resources to make true intrapreneurship possible.
- Forming cross-functional and inter-departmental committees to encourage collaboration and teamwork while maintaining informal channels through which the final decisions are made.

These technical ways of reducing the organization's levels of rigidity and control are not sustainable. They create the illusion that progress is being made in regard to the five structural variables, but they only deflect attention from the real and necessary adaptive work.

As with purpose and strategy, there is an antidote to the tendency toward avoidance. In the case of structure, the antidote is asking, "What would you do?" This question attacks the very foundation of the command-and-control paradigm, and the default behaviors that come with it.

Imagine a team meeting in which the boss presents a problem he perceives and, instead of giving instructions on what to do about it, asks for people's opinions, both in terms of diagnosis and action steps. He does this with true curiosity and a readiness to learn from his subordinates rather than wanting them to guess what might already be in his mind. The immediate effect should be to generate a better understanding of the problem and a more comprehensive response along with a higher level of engagement from the team. When this practice of giving the work back — putting responsibility on people's shoulders — is repeated, the long-term effect will be that people will feel more empowered to take initiative. They'll gradually internalize the criteria by which the organization makes decisions and come to realize that, in doing adaptive work, the boss may not always have the perfect answer.

A similar effect is attained in the U.S. Marines by providing the "commander's intent" as a way of conveying the criteria for making decisions and the idea that the commander might not have the perfect answer to the situation the soldiers are facing on the battlefield. These messages empower the Marines on the ground to make the decisions needed in the heat of battle, when there is no time to convene a team meeting.

In more typical business situations in which the pressure is less intense, asking "What would you do?" will end up reducing rigidity and introducing more flexibility to the company's structure. What might be time-consuming in the beginning will be time-saving in the end, because this practice will help produce more decentralization, more flexibility, more opportunities for straightforward conversations, more intrapreneurship, and more networking — all practices that lead to faster, smarter, and more effective decision making throughout the organization.

CHAPTER 7

CULTURE: THE ORGANIZATION'S BLOOD

If people in your organization tend to avoid problems rather than face them, you have a problem. And that problem is likely connected to culture.

Blood flows throughout the human body, pumped by the heart to the brain, to the fingers, to the toes, and to every major organ of the biological system. Blood is an essential component of the body, which could not exist without it.

Culture plays a similar role in a social system. Every nation, organization, and family has a culture of its own, invisible but helping to shape the values and norms that drive people's attitudes and behaviors. Sometimes those values and norms are explicitly defined and codified, as in most large corporations, but often they are implicit. Families do not write down the values they live by, but they are there, connected to the values of a larger system and shaping the way family members interact with one another.

GOOGLE AND LATAM AIRLINES: TWO KINDS OF ADAPTIVE CULTURES

Google is a company in which culture has been consciously studied and managed almost from the beginning. The prospectus for Google's 2004 initial public offering included a cover letter from founders Larry Page and Sergey Brin, which began, "Google is not a conventional company. We do not intend to become one."[54] A year later, at a time when Google's headcount was still relatively small and international operations were just taking off, two official documents — "Our Philosophy" and "The Golden Rules" — explicitly stated the values on which the company was being built. These included the belief that getting the best out of knowledge workers was the key to Google's success, and that this becomes possible when creativity is encouraged, when collaboration is built in, when decisions are consensus-based rather than imposed, when information is made available to everyone, when serious work can be done in a fun environment, and when there is constant dissatisfaction with the status quo.

Some observations from Google's employees reveal the degree to which these publicly espoused norms have become the reality of life in the company: "Google has a cultural aversion to top-down management." "The Google decision-making model breaks down if people are not collaborative. Someone who is very opinionated has a hard time working here without getting frustrated." "Google employees don't like to be told how to do something … this is seen as micromanaging. People would rather be mentored than managed." "We believe in the wisdom of crowds, and performance reviews is one of the many areas in which this philosophy drives our actions." "If you have an idea, you are encouraged to take the initiative and run with it." "I actually feel more entrepreneurial here than I did at my own company." "We want lunch lines to be long enough so that people bump into each other, but not so long that we are wasting employees' time." And because Google's culture is considered such an important asset, "there are many smart people that don't get hired because they don't fit culturally with the organization."[55]

Unlike Google, LAN Airlines did not consciously set out to build a culture. When the Cueto family took control in 1994, the company had many non-official declared subcultures struggling for survival and dominance, inherited from decades of state ownership combined with recent shifts in private ownership. The Cuetos added their own way of doing things, developed at FastAir, and the merger with Ladeco followed a bit later, bringing in yet another mix of cultural values and attitudes. Nonetheless, a strong culture started to emerge after a few years, based on the personal attitudes and behaviors of the young managers who arrived from FastAir and others who were later recruited. Most came from a similar cultural background and had similar styles, so that over time the values and norms that guided their behaviors permeated the organization. "Instead of asking for permission, ask for forgiveness" became a deeply rooted behavioral trait. So did the habit of saying things straight, with no ambiguity. LAN's young managers had no fear, were ambitious and competitive, and were hands-on people ready to perform whatever task was needed at any given moment. And, despite the formal hierarchy in which they operated, they related to one another in an informal, horizontal mode rather than allowing barriers to slow their decisions. Only a decade later, when the organization became more complex, did LAN's executives begin to explicitly address the issue of corporate culture.

Of course, Google and LATAM Airlines are in different industries that are generally characterized by different kinds of organizations — innovative in the case of Google, action-driven in the case of LATAM. Nonetheless, both companies share distinctive traits that make them more adaptive. Both are inclined to face adaptive challenges instead of avoiding them. This means that problems are surfaced and opportunities are seized, that there is always space for improvement, that people feel responsible, that losses are assumed, and that external feedback is heard. An organization with this type of culture will thrive better than others, just as societies with cultures that share these traits have thrived better than others since the very beginning of civilization.[56]

By contrast, cultural characteristics help to account for the problems experienced by Saab Automobile as well as the company's ultimate extinction. Perfectionism, innovation, and uniqueness were deeply held values in the company, explaining the quality of the cars it produced. The downside of these values, however, was arrogance and stubbornness, which led managers and engineers to avoid rather than address the adaptive challenges they faced long before GM took control. Because Saab's culture was so inward looking and impermeable, it ended up limiting the organization's adaptive capacity, leading company managers to ignore the signals that were coming from outside and then to disown the responsibility for responding to those signals.

An organization whose culture encourages facing challenges rather than avoiding them is one that lives with disequilibrium and tension. This requires a strong holding environment, as we saw in chapter 1, which from a cultural standpoint is associated with high levels of trust. When trust is lacking, people fall back on intense individualism, limiting collaboration, creativity, learning, and responsibility. These are all critical cultural values that enhance the adaptive capacity of an organization or a society.[57]

FIVE KEY VARIABLES: INDEPENDENT JUDGMENT, SHARED RESPONSIBILITY, OPENNESS, LEARNING, TRUST

Within the dimension of culture are five key variables that you need to think about and measure in pursuing greater adaptive capacity:

1. The exercise of *independent judgment* by those within the organization
2. A sense of *shared responsibility for the organization*
3. *Openness to disagreement* within the organization
4. A high capacity for *learning, especially from mistakes and failure*
5. *Trust*, both among employees and between employees and the authorities

If we go back to Figure 1-1, these variables can increase your organization's adaptive capacity by strengthening the holding environment, enhancing the responsiveness, or both.

Let's consider these variables one by one.[58]

Independent judgment. As we've discussed, human societies long ago accepted the idea that authorities have the answers and provide the solutions. The effect of this belief has been dependence on and deference to authority, even within decentralized structures — in other words, a lack of independent judgment. Of course, the degree to which this happens varies among cultures and has been shrinking in the knowledge era, when much more adaptive work is required.

At Google, independent judgment is valued; people are encouraged to act without expecting instructions and to disagree with the authorities when necessary. These values come naturally in an innovative kind of organization founded in an individualistic Anglo-Saxon culture and permeated by Millennials. Google's challenge is to take advantage of its high degree of individual autonomy in ways that make collective sense.

By contrast, LATAM Airlines exhibits a lower level of independent judgment, which is understandable in an action-driven kind of organization founded and operated in a Latin American culture and permeated by members of Generation X. An important challenge for LATAM is to encourage as many people as possible, in all levels of the organization, to feel authorized to exercise leadership and go beyond their job descriptions when dictated by their best independent judgment, a trait that existed in LAN but that has partially faded away as the organization has grown internationally, especially after the merger with TAM.

This is essential for any organization that needs to meet adaptive challenges, whether large, such as successfully implementing a strategic merger with another airline, or small, such as improving the service quality on flights or even simply keeping the ticket counters neat and clean. The more that people feel authorized to think for themselves, the more challenges will be addressed and progress attained. For this virtuous cycle to begin, authorities have to start sending the correct signals, encouraging people to take the initiative and to express their opinions.

Independent judgment is a variable that has important weight in increasing an organization's adaptive capacity; it does so by enhancing its responsiveness, because it enables people to express their points of view and concerns rather than defer to authorities.

When thinking about your own organization, ask yourself, "Do our authorities provide space for open discussion in meetings, asking for people's input and acknowledging their initiative?" and "How do our authorities react when their point of view is questioned by lower-ranking employees?"

Shared responsibility for the organization. The desire to establish and protect silos, fiefdoms, and turf constitutes a disease that has helped to kill many organizations. When people focus solely on the performance of their own team or the results of their own department or division, the big picture is lost amid all sorts of misunderstandings, conflicts, and lost opportunities. The final effect is often massive avoidance in the form of blaming others for the organization's problems due to a lack of willingness to acknowledge personal contributions to the mess.

Reward systems play an important role here. Bonuses, stock options, and other incentives should be based at least in part on the performance of the company as a whole so as to encourage a sense of shared responsibility for the entire organization. Equally important are role definitions and organizational designs, which can favor turf-protecting behavior when they are too rigid. But most important of all is the cultural trait of mutual understanding — the willingness of employees to step into one another's shoes and comprehend one another's perspective.

An organization in which this attitude is lacking may come to resemble a political system in which the national interest takes a back seat to party advantage. This is an unfortunate side effect of democracy, in which competition for power is a built-in element, designed to minimize corruption and provide opportunities for representing every point of view. In most companies, however, open competition for power is not encouraged, which makes it much easier (at least in theory) to promote values like collective responsibility and collaboration, which prioritize the organization's well-being rather than that of any faction. Collaboration — which is the opposite of silo behavior — is in fact a fundamental trait for boosting adaptive capacity, because open and generous interaction among employees allows the company to seize opportunities that would otherwise be missed. But collaboration doesn't come naturally; it can be triggered only when there is a mutual sense of belonging to something that is larger than your own silo, along with the realization that what is good for another person is also good for me. When this happens, there is a sense of shared responsibility for the whole, and collaboration becomes possible.

This feeling of shared responsibility for the organization increases its adaptive capacity by both strengthening the holding environment and enhancing the responsiveness. When people feel they belong together, they remain together and they build together.

When thinking about your own organization, ask yourself, "Do our people share resources, ideas, insights and lessons across functional and other boundaries?" and "How often do our people blame other employees or departments for the problems they face?"

Openness to disagreement. In 1989, when GM acquired 50 percent of Saab Automobile, managers in both companies had reasons to be enthusiastic about the future. The Swedish company had found a partner with the resources to promote growth and profitability, and the American giant had acquired a brand to compete with other high-quality European cars. The initial meetings with people from both sides were easygoing, touching on general topics about vision and plans. But soon, as the discussions became more concrete, differences in ideas, values, styles, expectations, commitments, and assumptions emerged.

Generally these differences were discussed outside the formal meetings, at the coffee machine or elsewhere, and only among those who came from the same company. Typically, the Swedes would complain about their partner's blindness to what Saab was all about, and the Americans would complain about their partner's stubbornness regarding the changes needed to make the firm profitable. When these complaints were aired publicly, the relationship became strained. The result? The differences were never really addressed, adaptive work on both sides was avoided, the distance between the partners increased, and Saab lost money for almost twenty years, including a decade during which GM owned 100 percent of the business.

Differences among people are part of everyday life, in the organizational context and beyond. We can choose to have a conversation about those differences, openly acknowledging the elephants in the room (discussed in Chapter 3), or we can choose to avoid such discussion, confining the topic to our own heads or to quiet talks with those who share our perspective. The first alternative means facing the implied adaptive challenge; the second alternative means avoiding it. However, if we decide to have the conversation, we need not only the necessary courage to do it but also the ability to hold people in that difficult space of the conversation.

When an organization values frankness, disagreement, and diversity, when people who raise hard questions are not labeled as troublemakers, and when the focus is on the problem rather than on the person, acknowledging the elephants in the room and addressing the underlying issues becomes much easier. Diversity has no value in itself; its value comes from the interaction among the different perspectives it embodies, which is only possible when there is openness to disagreement and the elephants are acknowledged. Therefore an organization should bring in a diverse group of people, but it should also ensure that the richness they provide can be expressed through an openness to disagreement. Otherwise, the potential of that diversity for increasing the organization's adaptive capacity will be lost.

The stronger this cultural trait is, the more adaptive the organization will be, in this case enhancing its responsiveness as more divergent voices are heard.

When thinking about your own organization, ask yourself, "How much time do our people spend sharing rumors and gossip?" and "Do our people voice the problems they perceive instead of remaining quiet about them?"

Learning, especially from mistakes and failure. As we've seen, adaptation is based on experimentation, which is nature's chief tool for permitting organisms to learn new ways to adapt and thrive.

The very origins of Google illustrate this point. Two PhD students in the computer science department at Stanford University were experimenting with different algorithms for ranking Internet search results. They learned from each experiment, produced adaptations to the formula, and finally devised an algorithm that would take them from the intellectual environment to the business arena. Google was born, and its history ever since has been a tale of continued experimentation, learning, and adaptation.

Of course, experimentation and learning at the individual level or within small groups is one thing, but institutionalizing learning as an essential aspect of an organization's culture is quite another. In particular, developing the willingness to embrace the most valuable and difficult type of learning — the learning that comes from failure — is difficult for many organizations. Google has striven to get there, as employee testimonies like this one reveal: "I know it may sound like a cliché, but failure is really OK here. I have heard our vice president tell a story in which she made a mistake that cost Google in the vicinity of a million dollars. When she admitted the mistake to Larry [Page], he told her that they would rather she make a mistake in moving too fast than make no mistakes and move too slow."[59] Of course, an essential element in such "good mistakes" is studying and explaining why the mistake occurred, which makes it possible for the entire organization to learn from a single employee's failure.

For this to happen, individuals need to be open and humble enough to learn from others; they also need to be generous and vulnerable enough to share their own learning with others, including the learning that comes from failure. Authorities must model these attitudes, especially by acknowledging their own mistakes. If the organization's authorities hide their failures or blame others for them, people through the company will do the same, guaranteeing that adaptive problems will be avoided rather than faced.

The readiness to learn, especially from mistakes and failure, increases the adaptive capacity of an organization by enhancing its responsiveness, since it allows team members to absorb and apply the lessons that come from experimentation.

When thinking about your own organization, ask yourself, "Do our people devote time to getting together and debriefing themselves on experiences that can generate organizational learning?" and "Are failures and mistakes easily acknowledged and used as a source of organizational learning?

Trust. The four previous variables in the dimension of culture help to create and maintain the tension necessary for challenges to be faced rather than avoided. But this tension requires a container that can keep people together despite the difficulty of openly acknowledging and exploring problems and the discomfort this behavior may create.

Trust is the most important cultural factor in building the necessary holding environment. Trust derives from predictability and consistency in the two domains of professional competency and shared values. For example, Google employees tend to trust one another because they know that having been hired by Google they are all professionally competent and share similar values. This is horizontal trust. At the same time, they also trust their authorities, because those authorities have demonstrated through their own behavior (as well as through Google's remarkable success) that they embody those same promises of professional competency and personal values. This is vertical trust.

Described this way, trust may sound like a simple matter. But gaining other people's trust is hard work, especially when expectations about competencies and values are not sufficiently aligned in the organization. When this happens, individuals, especially authorities, can expect to be trusted by some, distrusted by others, and subject to permanent scrutiny by still others (often the largest group). Under these circumstances, an employee who acknowledges the elephants in the room or an authority who gives the work back to stimulate his team's initiative may earn his colleagues' mistrust, especially if values like frankness and empowerment are not sufficiently ingrained in the organization's culture. This is why aligning values through consciously working the culture is of such paramount importance for organizational authorities.

The main effect of horizontal trust is bonding, which triggers the willingness to step into other people's shoes, to understand them, and to collaborate with them. The main effect of vertical trust is purpose reaffirmation, which triggers the willingness to engage in the organization and add value to it. Both are critical in providing the holding environment necessary when disequilibrium is high and adaptive work is needed.[60]

As we've seen, trust increases an organization's adaptive capacity by strengthening its holding environment — in fact, trust is one of the main factors involved in creating a strong holding environment.

When thinking about your own organization, ask yourself, "Is enough work being done to align people to the organization's values and the required level of competencies?" and "Are vertical trust and horizontal trust issues that our top executives and our executive committee are focused on?"

CULTURE IN VARIOUS KINDS OF ORGANIZATIONS

Every organization, large or small, has a culture of its own, which can either increase or diminish the organization's adaptive capacity. When the implicit norms that govern relationships among people dictate lowering one's voice, hiding problems, focusing solely on one's own sphere of activity, avoiding risk-taking, following orders without judging them, blaming others, and restraining open conversation, then adaptive challenges will be avoided rather than faced.

Interestingly, the same kinds of non-adaptive cultural traits can be found in societies, nations, families, and individuals, some of whom are more inclined to avoid adaptive challenges than to face them. But culture is not destiny. Cultural traits can be changed, especially in organizations that can recruit new employees, discharge others, and work on improving the internal dynamics among people using the five variables. This is something that is not feasible for a single person and is extremely difficult when it comes to politics at the national level, but it's possible.

The first step is to know the specific traits your company needs to work on in order to have a culture that will increase adaptive capacity. Start by going back to Figure 2-2 and use the kind of organization your industry is closest to as a benchmark.

Generally speaking, we expect innovative and action-driven organizations to have cultures that are relatively open to confronting challenges; after all, they would not survive otherwise given the instability of the environments they live in. However, innovative organizations will usually have more people who are prone to addressing adaptive challenges since the very nature of their work is more adaptive, complex, and talent-oriented. People in an innovative organization are likely to jump forward to confront challenges due to interior tension, whereas people in an action-driven organization will do so in response to an exterior pressure.

Communal and bureaucratic organizations, in turn, will have cultures more devoted to avoiding challenges, the former because of the fear of damaging personal relationships or being marginalized by the group when stepping forward; the latter because their very nature is to be defensive, acting only under duress.

To be more specific, look at the five variables related to the culture dimension and see how they would look for each kind of organization. The knobs of the culture equalizer are shown in Figure 7-1.

Figure 7-1. The culture equalizer

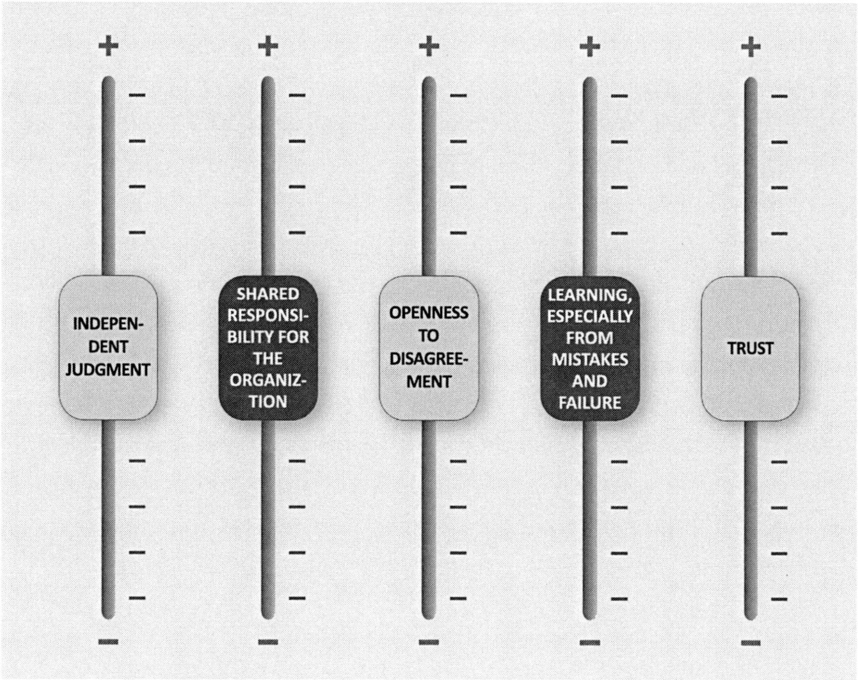

In an innovative organization, all five knobs will be in the upper range of the equalizer, since the big underlying goal is to maximize individuals' potential, which represents the ultimate competitive advantage of a company that performs a lot of adaptive work and is subject to the demands of an unstable environment. Indeed, past a certain stage of development, culture becomes more important than strategy and structure for this kind of organization.

Action-driven organizations are, in the extreme, exactly the opposite — all five knobs are in the lower range. When the work to be done is technical and the organization is rather small, this system works quite well, and because the voice of the authority is heard loud and clear, the company moves quickly enough to cope with the unstable environment. The challenge is when the organization becomes more complex and when more adaptive challenges emerge, dragging the company upward in Figure 2-2. The knobs will have to start moving toward the mid-range; otherwise the organization's survival may be at risk.

Because they function in stable environments, bureaucratic organizations have structures that do not change much, and because they do technical work, delegation is easy to implement. This means that role definitions can be very precise, making independent judgment more frequent than in action-driven organizations. In the same way, trust will be in the mid-range because people have more time to get to know one another and build strong relationships. The rest of the knobs will rank in the lower range, since there is no force or incentive moving people to leave their comfort zone.

Communal organizations operate closer to the mid-range in all five culture variables. However, openness to disagreement tends to be below the mid-range, and the other four knobs tend to be above. Trust might well be in the upper range because of the high levels of bonding and purpose, but the consequent strong holding environment would typically be wasted rather than generate more disequilibrium and progress. This happens, as we saw in Chapter 2, because the holding environment becomes an end in itself and the fear of putting relationships at risk is too deep.

HOW COMPANIES IGNORE THE IMPORTANCE OF CULTURE, AND THE POWER OF ASKING "WHAT IS THE PROBLEM REALLY ABOUT?"

As individuals, we are used to training our brains, our skeletons, our hearts, and even our souls. We do intellectual work to keep our brains sharp; we stretch and bend to keep our skeletons flexible; we do aerobic exercises to keep our hearts strong; and we "feed our souls" (as the saying goes) through a variety of artistic, social, spiritual, and moral activities. But we are not used to doing anything to keep our blood healthy, except perhaps for taking medications when a doctor warns us that we are suffering from a condition like high cholesterol or hypoglycemia.

In a somewhat similar way, culture is often neglected in organizations. Top executives are used to devoting attention to the organization's strategy and structure, and increasingly to its purpose and its talent (as we shall see in Chapter 8). But culture typically lags behind — not because executives fail to recognize its existence or its importance, but because they don't know how to deal with it.

We've seen how culture played a role in the demise of Saab Automobile. Would the story have been different if, for example, specific efforts had been made to build trust between the executives of Saab and GM as a basis for acknowledging the elephants in the room instead of talking about them in private and blaming others? It is likely that the answer is yes, because more frank conversations would have taken place about the company's strategy, including both what it is and how to do it, and the tradeoffs between identity and costs would have been addressed. Instead, they skipped all this and went directly to the technical task in front of them.

Lou Gerstner avoided this mistake. He spent a year focusing on IBM's culture, which he understood was crucial. He knew that unless he reoriented the organization toward customers, technical work alone would not save IBM. In Jack Welch's words, "A company can boost productivity by restructuring, removing bureaucracy, and downsizing, but it cannot sustain high productivity without culture change."[61]

The default behavior of traditional managers is to simply ignore cultural issues, staying in the world of elements that can be easily measured. Some managers even contend that "what cannot be measured does not exist." They're motivated by their fear of driving the organization into terrain where they feel uncomfortable, incompetent, and devoid of credibility. They may talk about culture from time to time, but they consistently underestimate it.

Some of the most common avoidance mechanisms used to treat culture as more technical than adaptive include:

- Confusing culture with identity, which can lead top executives to reinforce the sense of belonging by strengthening the boundaries between "us" and "them." This will lessen the organization's adaptive capacity, making it more self-oriented and blind to external changes.
- Confusing culture with organizational climate, which refers to people's mood in a specific period of time. Fixing the climate has little to do with changing culture; indeed, climate may worsen when the organization is doing adaptive work on culture.
- Deferring all issues related to culture to the human resources department — a mistake, because culture cannot be addressed without the involvement of the CEO, whose behavior is the most visible and powerful model presented to employees.
- Limiting the cultural work to defining a set of organizational values, which may be declared but not ingrained and therefore are not truly part of the culture.
- Addressing cultural gaps through training workshops aimed at developing individuals' competencies, without a systemic approach that would identify and address concrete and well-defined cultural challenges.

These technical ways of addressing the organization's culture miss the point, because in the end they don't touch the culture or any of the five variables that I've described. The only effect is to allow top executives to say that they care about culture, even as the company neglects this critical resource for increasing its adaptive capacity.

Fortunately, as with the previous dimensions, there is an antidote against this kind of avoidance that can bring culture to the attention of top executives. The antidote is asking, "What is the problem really about?" This question, repeated as often as necessary, forces people to think about the causes of the problem, not just the symptoms. Those causes are often related to values and behaviors — that is, to culture.

Imagine the CEO of a medium-size company who is concerned about an increase in customers' quality complaints for which no satisfactory explanation has been provided. He decides to hold a meeting with people from the company's operations, marketing, and sales departments, and begins by saying: "It seems we have a problem with our product quality. What is going on?"

The sales manager is the first to respond. "I saw the figures in the customer survey and passed the information to operations, but I haven't heard anything back."

An operations executive responds, "Yes, I got your email, and we discussed the issue in our staff meeting. My team members agree that the problem goes back to our advertising, which exaggerates our product's capabilities."

Now a marketing manager jumps into the conversation. "Nobody ever raised that issue before!"

"That's just because you never asked for our opinion," answers the operations executive.

"Well, if you ask me," the sales manager interjects, "the problem is unrealistic sales targets. We had to make all kinds of promises to push the product out the door. No wonder people are unhappy with it now!"

When the CEO gets answers like these, he should immediately realize that the problem is not fundamentally about a flawed product, a poor advertising campaign, or excessive sales targets. It's about certain dynamics in the company that are rooted in cultural traits: a lack of shared responsibility for the organization, an unwillingness to address uncomfortable issues openly, and a general lack of trust. Repeatedly asking "What is the problem really about?" may eventually force these cultural issues out into the open where they can be dealt with.

Understanding the cause of a problem is not enough, but it is a good beginning. Not all the problems of an organization have a cultural cause, of course, but many do, and asking questions that force the analysis can prevent the organization's members from ignoring this fact.

CHAPTER 8

TALENT: THE ORGANIZATION'S HEART

If people in your organization don't embody the principles and ideals that supposedly define what the organization is and how it behaves, you have a problem. And that problem is likely connected to talent.

From ancient times, the heart has always been considered the body's most essential organ. In fact, the words "heart" and "core" come from the same Indo-European root, *kerd*.[62] It is the heart that pumps the blood that irrigates every organ in the body, providing them with nutrients and allowing them to function.

The same happens with talent in an organization. We can talk about purpose, strategy, structure, and culture, but these are only abstract concepts without people to make them real. Talent must be the incarnation of those four dimensions. For a company to be more adaptive, there must be a group of individuals who infuse meaning, who think, who encourage flexibility, and who tackle the challenges they face. The larger this group, the more adaptive the organization.

GE, NETFLIX, AND FC BARCELONA: THREE GREAT DEVELOPERS OF ADAPTIVE TALENT

GE was once known as the most prominent "leadership factory" in the world. The company founded the first corporate university at Crotonville,

New York, in the mid-1950s — a symbol of the importance that GE places on human capital development. On his retirement, CEO Jack Welch said, "My main job was developing talent. I was a gardener providing water and other nourishment to our top 750 people. Of course, I had to pull out some weeds, too."[63] He also said, "Nothing matters more in winning than getting the right people on the field. All the clever strategies and advanced technologies in the world are not effective without great people to put them to work."[64] It was Jack Welch who popularized the idea that organizations, in the end, are nothing more or less than the talent they are able to attract and mobilize — a truth that was not so obvious in the 1980s, when most of the business world still lived under the industrial paradigm.

GE also understood that talent development must evolve to meet the needs of a changing world. In 2009, Susan Peters, then head of the company's leadership training, started aggressively rethinking the program, including the famous facility at Crotonville itself:

> We now recognize that external focus is more multifaceted than simply serving the customer, that other stakeholders have to be considered. We talk about how to get and apply external knowledge, how to lead in ambiguous situations, how to listen actively, and the whole idea of collaboration.... We are physically changing the buildings, to make it better for teams. A large kitchen has been installed, so teams can cook together with all the messiness and egalitarian spirit involved. And then there's the building known around campus as the "White House," which dates back to the 1950s. It's where executives would go after dinner to have a drink. We're gutting it, replacing it with a university-like all-day coffeehouse.[65]

Today, Google sets the benchmark for talent developing at the beginning of the twenty-first century. As a human resources manager at Google affirmed, "We believe that we hire people who are well-intentioned, curious and aware, and most have the capacity to self-govern with the help of their peers."[66]

Netflix is another company where talent is recognized as a key factor to adapt and thrive. Founded in 1997 in California as an online DVD rental company (one of many at that time), it quickly evolved as an innovative business model of monthly flat-fee unlimited rentals without due dates, late penalties, shipping or handling charges. Today it is the world's leading Internet subscription service for enjoying movies and television shows streamed over all different sorts of technological devices, and it has successfully entered the business of developing original films and series, even winning Emmy and Academy awards for some of its first productions. And when it comes to people, the model is pretty straightforward, as stated by co-founder and CEO Reed Hastings, who wants to "increase employee freedom as we grow, rather than limit it, to continue to attract and nourish innovative people, so we have a better chance of long-term continued success."

To make this possible, Netflix continually reinforces nine behaviors and skills that promote adaptability: judgment, communication, impact, curiosity, innovation, courage, passion, honesty, and selflessness. This is why, from a structure approach, Netflix has only two types of rules for controlling people: those designed to prevent irrevocable disaster and those designed to deal with moral, ethical, and legal issues. There is no vacation policy, no tracking of work schedules, and no expense or travel policy, for example. As the Netflix "Reference Guide on our Freedom and Responsibility Culture" says: "Avoid chaos as you grow with ever more high performance people, not with rules," because "Flexibility is more important than efficiency in the long run."[67]

The relationship between talent and performance is especially visible in sports, in which the Barcelona football team provides one of the best examples in history of a team that has made the most of its members' exceptional skills. The challenge is not merely bringing good players into the organization, but making them embody and project the underlying properties of the team's purpose, strategy, structure, and culture. Most professional sport teams are the sum of a group of more or less skilled individuals who play together for rather short periods of time, trying to deploy a collective scheme in each game. The teams that succeed are those that exhibit the highest aggregate competencies while competing, which depends on both the individual abilities and the way the collective dynamic takes advantage of them.

Unlike its archrival Real Madrid, in the early 2000s Barcelona started developing a strategy to rely less on buying expensive and already acclaimed players and more on developing the young players from the club's juvenile divisions — for example, Lionel Messi, considered one of the best players in soccer history, who arrived at the club from Argentina when he was only thirteen years old. It was not just a matter of resources, but rather of creating a real team rather than a group of exceptional players. This provided the opportunity to develop strong bonds and values, and, ultimately, to consciously work on building a culture.

The strategy started yielding fruit in 2008, when Josep Guardiola, a former Barcelona player with only one year of experience coaching Barcelona's B-team in the third division, was named the coach of the main team. During his four seasons in the position, Barcelona became the best soccer team ever, winning 14 titles and becoming the base of the Spanish national team that won the World Cup in 2010.

Talent, then, is more than having skilled people; it is having skilled people who embody the qualities of a more adaptive organization. Attracting, developing, and retaining talent is not therefore something aimed at a special group of individuals who have exceptional competencies or occupy key positions, but at all employees. Organizations need as many people as possible that have or can develop the technical competencies of the function they perform and, at the same time, embody the qualities of the organization they aspire to become.

FIVE KEY VARIABLES: IDENTIFICATION, RIPENING, FEEDBACK, CHALLENGE, MODELS

Within the dimension of talent are five key variables you need to think about and measure in pursuing greater adaptive capacity:

1. A system for *identification* of employees who will enhance your adaptive capacity
2. A readiness to support the *ripening* process in employees as they grow and develop
3. A system and a culture that supports the provision of honest *feedback*
4. A determination to provide ever-changing *challenge* for talented employees
5. *Models* who represent the kinds of talent the organization needs

If we go back to Figure 1-1, these variables can increase your organization's adaptive capacity by strengthening the holding environment, enhancing the responsiveness, or both. Let's consider these variables one by one.

Identification. Identifying talent is much more than identifying smart or competent people. It is identifying people who will make the organization more adaptive. This demands, in the first place, that you define the traits that will increase your company's adaptive capacity, given the kind of organization it is closest to. In doing this, the variables related to each of the previous four dimensions are a useful guide. Once you have those definitions, they need to be translated into a set of attitudes and behaviors that you expect all of your employees to embody.

Reed Hastings of Netflix knew early on that he wanted to build an organization that would be different from other movie rental companies. He did not know the exact business model that would make Netflix successful, but he anticipated that doing things differently within the organization would make a difference in the business. He believed in the benefits of being as adaptive as possible, and he realized that this meant granting freedom to employees. With these basic ideas in mind, he started experimenting in order to arrive at a successful organizational model. Ideas were refined over time, and once executives gained clarity about the organization they wanted, a set of behaviors and skills were defined. That list of nine traits became the key to hiring people, focusing employee development efforts, evaluating and promoting individuals, and, when necessary, discharging them.

Identifying the right talent will increase an organization's adaptive capacity by enhancing its responsiveness, because the organization will seek out and hire employees who are especially focused on looking for opportunities and mobilizing resources toward them.

When thinking about your own organization, ask yourself, "Is there a clear definition of attitudes and behaviors that our company expects from employees and that are connected to continually increasing its adaptive capacity?" and "Is there a policy being applied to replace those employees who do not fit the definition?"

Ripening. Organizations evolve through facing their adaptive challenges rather than avoiding them. This is difficult work, as we have seen, and they have to strive for a while — sometimes a long time — before they start seeing the fruits. The same is true for individuals. We evolve by facing adaptive challenges, but we never get it right immediately. There is a learning process that takes some time.

Companies need to recognize and address this reality by first challenging their employees, then supporting them in the ripening process. There are many ways to do this, starting with formal training in the technical skills that the new challenge may require. But the key is accompanying them along the way, using tools like internal workshops, mentoring, coaching, peer and group consulting, and sponsoring. The process demands patience and reinforcement, especially from bosses, which provide the emotional container that permits an employee to give his or her best.

Top soccer players often have trouble adapting to a new team. It is usually not because they need to develop new technical skills but because they have to get used to a different play scheme and sometimes a different position; they have to gain acceptance from their teammates and build new relationships; and they have to adapt to living in a new city or country, and even learning a new language. A good coach will understand these difficulties and help the player ripen rather than cut him off prematurely.

One of Netflix's predicaments is that "people who have been stars for us, and hit a bad patch, get a near term pass because we think they are likely to become stars for us again."[68] This is a neat way to acknowledge that even the most brilliant people need to learn; they may have a hard time when they assume a new position, take over a new project, join a new team, are given a new boss, or face a personal problem.

A company's challenge, therefore, is to help its people swim in rough waters, supporting them in the process rather than letting them drown. In Jack Welch's analogy, top executives must be the gardeners who help their people ripen and give the best fruits they're able to produce.

Supporting the ripening process of talent is an essential variable in increasing an organization's adaptive capacity. It does so by strengthening the holding environment. People appreciate a company that provides them the backing and time they need to grow, and they will want to remain there despite the difficulties and hard moments they may experience along the way.

When thinking about your own organization, ask yourself, "What are the tools that the company uses to support its employees' growth within the organization?" and "How are those tools connected to continually increasing our organization's adaptive capacity?"

Feedback. There is always a difference between the way we see ourselves and the way others see us. We are usually unaware of certain personal traits we have and their impact on other people. If we did not have those blind spots, we would be more conscious of the gaps in our professional and personal growth and would feel the tension we need to close those gaps.

Receiving feedback from others can help make us less blind. But being called upon to give feedback to someone else is not easy. Why risk saying something that could hurt or anger the other person and might backfire on you? For this reason, many people find it difficult to provide feedback, especially feedback that questions behavior rather than reinforcing it. Yet feedback that questions behavior is particularly valuable, since it enables employees to identify gaps and open spaces for improvement. An organization that can master the art of providing both kinds of feedback — especially feedback that questions behavior — can dramatically improve its adaptive capacity.

GE realized this in the late 1980s and made improvement of its feedback system one of its key organizational initiatives for augmenting talent performance. Among the feedback tools GE implemented were extensive management review meetings focused on the top 3,000 executives, the 360-degree evaluation, and the classification of employees in a two-dimensional grid according to their performance and values. Jack Welch himself would devote 70 percent of his time to these and other people issues.[69]

Whatever specific tools you choose, honest and straightforward feedback is one of the most effective ways to boost talent in a company. Feedback should in fact be considered a cultural trait related to learning rather than merely a tool. In the most adaptive organizations, feedback is not limited to evaluation processes but is part of daily life, occurring in all sorts of conversations and meetings. Welch created a culture around feedback that he considered one of his main legacies.

Honest feedback — especially the kind that makes people question themselves — increases an organization's adaptive capacity by enhancing its responsiveness, precisely because it enables employees to see what they haven't seen about themselves and their environments. Receiving and learning from this feedback advances their level of consciousness as well as that of the company.

When thinking about your own organization, ask yourself, "Is there a formal feedback process that includes one-on-one or group conversations and that puts emphasis on how each person embodies the qualities of a more adaptive organization?" and "Is there a culture that makes providing feedback a natural part of our day-to-day business operations?"

Challenge. Talent looks for a challenge, and facing challenges makes an organization thrive. This simple idea has an immense impact: if there are no challenges available, talent will depart and the organization will stagnate — and this reduces the number of challenges still further, creating a vicious cycle.

An employee who has the necessary technical skills and who has been successfully developing the qualities of the more adaptive organization the company wants to become needs to be put in the right place to push himself and the organization forward. And, of course, the "right place" may not be an existing position. Because an organization with high adaptive capacity is permanently evolving, new projects, initiatives, and challenges will continually emerge at all levels that require talent to be developed — a virtuous cycle.

Thus, an organization that wants to increase its adaptive capacity needs to understand individuals' motivations and open opportunities for them rather than design career paths that provide security. Likewise, rewards should be aligned to the value employees add rather than aligned to the time they have worked for the company.

Netflix is a good example of a company that works this way: "We develop people by giving them the opportunity to develop themselves, by surrounding them with stunning colleagues and giving them big challenges to work on. Mediocre colleagues or unchallenging work is what kills progress of a person's skills. . . . Career planning is not for us. Formalized development is rarely effective, and we don't try to do it."[70] This is one reason Netflix increasingly explores and develops new initiatives and businesses, making it hard to predict where it will end up one or two decades hence.

Of course, tackling challenges can lead to mistakes. In 2011, Reed Hastings announced that Netflix's DVD rental business would be split off as a subsidiary, forcing customers to pay separately — and significantly more — if they wanted both streaming and rentals. The effect was the loss of 800,000 subscribers and a 75 percent drop in the stock price. Netflix and Hastings promptly demonstrated their adaptive capacity. The company reversed the decision, and Hastings publicly acknowledged the mistake to his customers, asking for their forgiveness. The company quickly recovered and is now more successful than ever. The story vividly illustrates how the existence of permanent challenges increases the adaptive capacity of an organization by enhancing its responsiveness.

When thinking about your own organization, ask yourself, "Do we strive to understand the motivations and interests of individual employees, especially those most identified with the company?" and "Is there an inclination to continually search for new challenges as a way of opening opportunities for talent development?"

Models. Having talent means having people possessing the technical skills for the functions they perform and also possessing the qualities of a more adaptive organization. The more talent a company has, the higher its adaptive capacity. Raising the proportion of employees who can embody talent and increasing the quality of that talent is an ongoing effort that requires applying the prior four variables we've discussed to all talents, but especially to those who can model what the company needs.

At FC Barcelona, the team's coach, its captain, and its best players incarnate the values of the institution, thereby sending a clear signal to talent throughout the organization. To ensure this, since the mid-2000s Barcelona preferred to bet on players from its juvenile divisions who were raised with the institution's values. Barcelona supplemented this home-grown talent by signing a few additional promising young players rather than acquiring established star players from other teams who would be more difficult to align.

As Barcelona illustrates, the highest and most visible positions in a company should be filled with people who model the qualities of the more adaptive organization it aspires to become. The same is true of middle- and low-level authority positions, which are closer to most employees' daily activity. And when the company has employees who consistently behave in a way that is detrimental to those qualities, it may be necessary to make the difficult decision to terminate them, even if they are very talented in technical terms.

Models help to increase an organization's adaptive capacity by strengthening its holding environment, because they serve as magnets to other talents that can incarnate the values of the institution.

When thinking about your own organization, ask yourself, "Is there a group of people in different levels of our company who are aware of their modeling role and receive support to carry it out?" and "Does the CEO model the organizational qualities to which our company seeks to align our people?"

TALENT IN VARIOUS KINDS OF ORGANIZATIONS

If a company wants to increase its adaptive capacity, its people have to do the same — that is, they need to embody the qualities of a more adaptive organization in each of its four initial dimensions. Talent, the fifth dimension, is precisely that group of people who not only have the technical skills required by their function but also embody those adaptive qualities. The more talent an organization has, the more adaptive it becomes.

There is an important implication here that is often overlooked. An organization will not become more adaptive simply because the top management establishes a purpose, devises a strategy, designs a flexible structure, and defines new cultural values. This technical work is important, but even more important is the adaptive work of developing people who act with purpose, reflect, are flexible, and face challenges instead of avoiding them. This is developing talent, and it takes time, which is why increasing an organization's adaptive capacity is a gradual process that must be consciously driven.

GE, Barcelona, and Netflix, each in a different way, have faced the challenge of increasing its adaptive capacity by developing talent. All three knew they had to wait a few years to start reaping what they'd sown, and all three know that every day they have to keep developing talent to increase their adaptive capacity.

To see how much emphasis your company should put on developing talent to increase its adaptive capacity, go back to Figure 2-2 and use the kind of organization your industry is closest to as a benchmark.

Generally speaking, innovative and communal organizations will have to devote more attention to talent, since the adaptive nature of most of their work demands a higher proportion of people thinking, taking initiative, and making decisions.

By contrast, action-driven and bureaucratic organizations need to put less attention on talent, because most of the work they do is technical and thus can be performed by following the rules established in standard operating procedures or the instructions provided by the boss.

To be more specific, let's look at the five variables related to the talent dimension and see how they should look like for each kind of organization. The knobs for the talent equalizer are shown in Figure 8-1.

Figure 8-1. The talent equalizer

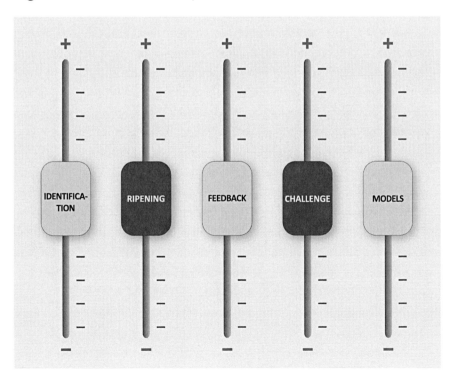

The talent dimension equalizer differs from the other four dimensions' equalizers in that its five knobs should generally move together. When a company pays attention to talent, it has to use all five variables to have an impact on its overall adaptive capacity. It is not enough to define what talent means and then hire or fire employees accordingly. You also have to do real work with people, pushing them to grow through a ripening process in which feedback is a critical element, providing them with new professional challenges that match their motivations as well as visible individuals who model the attitudes and behaviors being promoted. Of course, leveling these five variables is hard work that can be strategically paced and planned, but none of the five should be neglected for long.

An innovative organization should aim at having the five knobs in the upper range, not only because the kind of work it performs is mostly adaptive, but also because it has to move very fast given its unstable environment. Its goal should be to make all its employees talents, each embodying the qualities of an innovative organization in terms of purpose, strategy, structure, and culture.

Talent is almost equally important in a communal organization, though the lack of external pressure makes it less necessary to work this dimension so systematically. Since there is more time to respond and adapt, the organization can afford to do this in an informal way, resting on some talents who will do the job of developing others more than establishing procedures to ensure that this happens across the board. Therefore we should expect to find the knobs above the mid-range.

An action-driven organization has to move fast, but it does so by having a small group of people in top positions who make the decisions that will move the company forward in its unstable environment. Since most of the work is still technical — opening a new retail store, for example — implementation of those decisions does not require a great deal of talent. The action-driven company needs talent in the higher levels where decisions are made and in new projects that may be developed, but not throughout the whole organization. Therefore, we should expect to find the knobs close to the mid-range.

The bureaucratic organization is one where talent is less relevant. Most of the work it performs is technical and consists in following the rules with little or no discretion. And since there is little external pressure to change those rules, not even the people in top positions need a high adaptive capacity. Therefore, the talent knobs will be below the mid-range.

HOW COMPANIES AVOID THE TALENT CHALLENGE, AND THE POWER OF ASKING "WHY DO PEOPLE JOIN US? WHY DO THEY LEAVE?"

Whenever you go to the doctor, your blood pressure will be measured. The purpose is to check the condition of your heart, which your doctor knows is critical to your health. Yet between doctor visits, most of us think rather little about the condition of our hearts, in part because symptoms of heart trouble afflict us much less often than headaches, stomach aches, or backaches.

Something similar happens with talent in organizations. Outside consultants generally pay special attention to a company's talent because they know how critical talent is to any recommendations they may make. But most top executives take talent for granted and pay little attention to it in comparison to other issues. When faced with people issues, their default behavior is to approach these in terms of skills and positions, analyzing who should be in a specific post and who should not, rather than considering how the problems might be related to the manner in which the company tackles talent as a whole. The reason is clear: many managers intuitively realize that dealing with people may open a space for them to express opinions and feel empowered, creating problems the managers may feel incompetent to solve and that might even cause the managers to lose their own power.

Of course, since "talent" has become a prominent part of the business vocabulary, executives know they have to address it. But they find ways to resort to fake remedies, usually without realizing it, launching empty initiatives that give the false impression that progress is being made. The most common technical solutions that operate as mechanisms for avoiding the big adaptive challenge embodied in talent include:

- Developing evaluation systems that are ultimately used to decide on promotions and firings, not to provide feedback and help talents grow and ripen.

- Offering training programs or courses on technical skills, avoiding issues related to the organization itself and its challenges, especially those that focus on the qualities people should embody.
- Designing detailed career plans aimed at providing security rather than having individuals prepare their potential successors while opening all sorts of challenging opportunities to let talent strive and grow.
- Labeling a few people as talent, signaling that they are important to the company and should be retained. This creates rigidity, falsely suggests the idea that the whole issue of talent is being addressed, and sends equivocal signals to those who were not labeled as talent.
- Delegating talent issues to the human resources department, taking away the responsibility from the top executives who should be in charge of these issues.

These technical ways of addressing talent miss the crucial point of this dimension: working with talent to build a more adaptive organization. Evaluation systems, training programs, and even career plans may have their place. But it's important to recognize that they could be a waste of time if they are not connected to increasing the organization's adaptive capacity.

The antidote to avoidance in this dimension is to ask, "Why do people join us? Why do they leave?" These questions force a conversation about the broader issues of talent connected to the five variables we've analyzed, and especially about how the adaptive qualities the company aspires to are being embodied by employees, beyond paper definitions.

Imagine a meeting of the company's top team, where the human resources manager announces that several executives have left the firm in the past few weeks, adding that the process for filling those positions has already started. After the team briefly discusses the reasons given for the executives' departure and the profiles of some of the replacement candidates, they're ready to move to the next agenda item. But the operations manager interrupts and tries to go deeper: "Beyond the politically correct responses given by those who left, why are they really leaving the company? Is there a pattern here? Is there a problem we should be looking at?"

A question like this one, if tackled with the seriousness it deserves, can lead to an initial conversation about possible systemic issues that may hide beneath a spate of resignations — for example, a lack of challenging initiatives, a set of bosses who exercise too much control and limit the growth of individuals, or a lack of the collaboration needed to make things happen.

Someone else could further fuel the discussion by asking, "Why are candidates applying to work in this company?" Exploring this question could help the team better understand how the organization is being perceived and the gaps that should be addressed to attract the right people. Suppose the team discovers that candidates are applying mainly because of the benefits and security the company provides — think how different that would be from learning that they apply because of the professional challenges the company offers. This kind of conversation could help the top team look at talent in a more holistic way, not merely in terms of individuals and positions.

Organizations like GE, Netflix, and Barcelona know that talent is the key to their success — and not merely individual talents, but collective talent. Understanding this and making sure that the organization is permanently focused on the talent issue has been one of the secret weapons behind their success.

EPILOGUE: THE FOREST

It's not easy to see the forest emerging from the trackless tangle of trees in which we wander — or, to shift metaphors, to lead your troops on the battlefield and see the whole picture at the same time — but that is precisely the challenge faced by any top executive. Life can be seen as a process of increasing consciousness — consciousness about ourselves and about what surrounds us. The greater our consciousness, the more we can see, experience, accomplish, and enjoy — in life and in work. Yet, growing in consciousness is not an easy process. Typically it requires us to confront problems, weaknesses, and failings we'd rather keep as blind spots, thereby avoiding the challenges they represent. For this reason, some people make little progress in this process throughout their lifetimes, preferring to remain in their comfort zones despite the price of limited consciousness this entails. But others purposefully look for ways to become more conscious every day, challenging themselves, exploring their environments, and continually evolving.

In the pages of this book, you've encountered people at many places along this spectrum. Recall the engineer Jim, in Chapter 1, who evolved and grew in consciousness when his boss Sarah helped him recognize how his harsh management style had made his subordinates feel mistreated, resentful, and unmotivated. Or consider Bill Gates, whose mind expanded when some executives at Microsoft made him conscious of the Internet's potential to change the world. Or — at the other end of the spectrum — recall the newspaper publisher David Franco, who was unable to become fully conscious about the ways his default leadership behavior, once so successful, had caused him and his business to falter when circumstances changed.

I hope this book has played a positive role in your own journey toward greater consciousness, self-knowledge, and understanding. I hope that you can make sense of the many different trees around you and see them as a forest. My goal has been to help you become more conscious about your behaviors, attitudes, strengths, and weaknesses as an executive and about the dynamics of your organization, in the hope that this deeper awareness will enable you to better recognize and face the challenges before you. If that happens, you, your organization, and society as a whole will benefit.

Over time, most executives become very conscious about the business itself: the opportunities it enjoys, the competition it faces, the needs of its customers, the strategic challenges it must meet, and so on. But that is not enough. There is an organization that carries out the business, an organization composed of people, an organization with specific, ever-changing, complex dynamics, an organization whose workings can make the business a success or a failure. If the person running a company is like a helmsman guiding a boat through choppy seas, he needs to recognize that he has not one but two oars at his disposal — the business oar and the organizational oar. To be effective, an executive has to be conscious of both oars and use them both.

To wield the organizational oar skillfully, the executive must be guided by the idea of adaptive capacity. Every organizational decision should be oriented toward increasing that capacity, which is determined by the five crucial dimensions that make up the organization: its purpose, its strategy, its structure, its culture, and its talent. In this book, I've explained why this is so and sought to equip you with the distinctions and insights you need to answer the following four questions in regard to your own organization:

- How much adaptive capacity does it have?
- Is that adaptive capacity enough to meet the challenges it faces?
- How can its adaptive capacity be increased?
- What are the variables that may increase its adaptive capacity?

But just as organizations need to thrive by changing for a changing world, so do executives. If organizations are complex systems that tend to remain in equilibrium until forced to change by an adaptive challenge, so are people. And if there is an organizational adaptive capacity — the subject of this book — there is also a personal adaptive capacity. Many external and internal forces operate in each one of us. Sometimes those forces help us cope with the challenges we face, but sometimes they hinder our efforts, requiring us to struggle against them. At times, we even have to struggle against ourselves. That is when our individual adaptive capacities come into play, as executives and as people.[71]

Perhaps this could be the subject of another book. In the meantime, I hope that what you've learned here about the nature of adaptation and the tools we can use to enhance the adaptive capacity of our organizations will help you deal more effectively with the challenges you and we all face in a world that is growing more complex, more dynamic, and yet potentially more rewarding every day.

ACKNOWLEDGMENTS

Creating this book has been a difficult test of my own adaptive capacity. But certainly not only of mine. The patience of my wife, Catalina, was sorely tested during the lengthy writing process. But without her continual support, the job would never have been completed. Catalina was able to provide me with the holding environment I needed to carry out this demanding enterprise, as well as with many insights that challenged my thinking along the way. I will always be grateful to her.

As I mentioned in the Introduction, this book represents one piece of a collective effort initiated by Ronald Heifetz and Riley Sinder, and continued by Marty Linsky and Alexander Grashow as authors and co-authors in the field of adaptive leadership. Ronald Heifetz has been a true mentor to me since my years as a graduate student at the Harvard Kennedy School, and he was crucial in shaping and deepening some of the ideas presented in this book. He not only read the manuscript more than once but also met with me several times during the writing process, clarifying my thinking about specific topics and pushing me to go further. His continual encouragement and intellectual rigor made this book much better than it would have been otherwise.

Creating the initial framework of the book was not easy; there were so many issues to tackle and many possible angles from which to approach them. Alexander Grashow served as a valuable partner during this period, spending long hours with me in front of a whiteboard, week after week, helping me come up with a structure that would make sense and be helpful to executives.

My colleagues and partners in Latin America, both at Universidad Adolfo Ibáñez and at Cambridge Leadership Associates, assisted me greatly. Ignacio Martín Maruri was tireless in helping me refine my ideas as we tested them in our courses on Organizational Transformation. Diego Rodriguez and Alexandra Montenegro provided me with deep insights and encouraged me to think about the values that underlie the ideas presented in the book.

Stefan Reich, Rodolfo Rivarola, and Gregorio Etcheverry participated in a number of seminars and conversations in which the organizational framework developed here first emerged years ago.

Many other generous colleagues and businesspeople from around the world devoted time to reading the manuscript and providing me with feedback that greatly enhanced the final version. Among them, I would like to especially thank Carlos Eichholz, David Jackson, Tamas Landesz, Marcelino Elosua, César Piernavieja, Charles Burck, John Kador, Robert Kaplan, Armando Valdivieso, and José Luis Troncoso.

I am deeply grateful to my editor Karl Weber. He believed in this project when I first shared the manuscript with him. He helped me make the concepts and the stories clearer and more appealing to the reader, painstakingly transformed my prose into graceful English, and guided me through the publishing process.

Finally, I will always be indebted to my students and teaching assistants in the graduate courses I teach, as well as to the executives in the organizations I have worked with. They have inspired me to write this book and served as an endless source of learning for me, as I am sure they will continue to do in the future.

ABOUT THE AUTHOR

Juan Carlos Eichholz is a professor at the Business School of Adolfo Ibáñez University, where he has more than once been honored as the best professor in the school's MBA program. He is also the founding director of the Adaptive Leadership Center, which has served as a platform for bringing together an international community of professors and practitioners committed to help others and the larger society in making progress on their toughest challenges. Eichholz is also the founder and principal of CLA Consulting, which was born out of Cambridge Leadership Associates (CLA) to work with private companies as well as public and nonprofit institutions on mobilizing purposeful and adaptive change.

In addition to his work as an educator, international keynote speaker, and consultant, Eichholz has also been an active opinion maker as a columnist for *El Mercurio* newspaper in Chile and through his participation in television, radio, and newspaper debates. He is one of the founders of the Young Leaders initiative, which brings together the most influential Chileans under the age of thirty-five, and was appointed in 2006 as a Young Global Leader of the World Economic Forum. His interest in public and social issues led him to create and chair, in his younger years, two foundations.

Eichholz studied law at Universidad Católica de Chile and holds a Master's in Public Policy from Harvard University. Though he travels extensively, he is happiest at the home he shares with his wife and six children in Santiago de Chile.

NOTES

[1] Fred Vogelstein, "Why Google Scares Gates," *Fortune Magazine*, May 2, 2005.

[2] Ronald Heifetz, *Leadership Without Easy Answers* (Cambridge, MA: Harvard University Press, 1994); Ronald Heifetz and Marty Linsky, *Leadership on the Line* (Boston: Harvard Business School Press, 2002); Ronald Heifetz, Alexander Grashow, and Marty Linsky, *The Practice of Adaptive Leadership* (Boston: Harvard Business Press, 2009).

[3] The expression first appeared in the writings of professor Leon C. Megginson, as a paraphrase to Darwin's ideas: "According to Darwin's *Origin of Species*, it is not the most intellectual of the species that survives; it is not the strongest that survives; but the species that survives is the one that is able best to adapt and adjust to the changing environment in which it finds itself." Megginson, "Lessons from Europe for American Business," *Southwestern Social Science Quarterly* 44/1 (1963): 3–13, quote at 4.

[4] The story of David Franco and the *Home Star* is based on a real newspaper business, though the names and other identifying details have been changed.

[5] Randel Carlock and Elizabeth Florent-Treacy, *The HP-Compaq Merger: A Battle for the Heart and Soul of a Company* (Fontainebleau, FR: INSEAD, 2002).

[6] Ibid.

[7] Ibid.

[8] Niccolò Machiavelli, *The Prince* (New York: Bantam Books, 1966).

[9] Gary Hamel, "The Challenge Today: Changing the Rules of the Game," *Strategic Management in the Knowledge Economy* (New York: Wiley-VCH, 2005).

[10] Christopher A. Bartlett and Mec Wozny, *GE's Two-Decade Transformation: Jack Welch's Leadership* (Cambridge, MA: Harvard Business School, 2004).

[11] See Daniel Kahneman, Jack L. Knetsch and Richard H. Thaler, "Anomalies: The Endowment Effect, Loss Aversion, and Status Quo Bias," *Journal of Economic Perspectives* 5/1 (1991).

[12] Developed in collaboration with Ignacio Martín Maruri and adapted from Ronald A. Heifetz and Donald L. Laurie, "Mobilizing Adaptive Work: Beyond Visionary Leadership," in *The Leader's Change Handbook,* ed. Jay A. Conger, Gretchen M. Spitzer, and Edward E. Lawler III (San Francisco: Jossey-Bass, 1998).

[13] Colonel John R. Andrew Jr., "The Battle of An-Nasiriyah," *U.S. Marines in Battle* (Washington, DC: History Division, U.S. Marine Corps, 2009).

[14] For a deeper understanding of the roots and idea of authority, read Ronald Heifetz, *Leadership Without Easy Answers* (Cambridge, MA: Harvard University Press, 1994).

[15] The Spanish word *caudillo* makes reference to military or political authoritarian leaders, who tend to act in an arbitrary way, exceeding and weakening institutions. It is culturally interesting to note that the word does not exist in English, as "accountability" does not exist in Spanish.

[16] Adaptive work is at the core of this book, and the exercise of leadership is what allows it to take place, but it is not referred to in depth among these pages. For a more profound analysis, read Heifetz, Grashow, and Linsky, *The Practice of Adaptive Leadership.*

[17] Nando Parrado, *Miracle in the Andes* (New York: Random House, 2006).

[18] Matthias Holweg and Nick Oliver, *Who Killed Saab Automobile? Obituary of an Automotive Icon* (Cambridge: Judge Business School, University of Cambridge, 2012).

[19] Ibid.

[20] The development of this chart has been an evolutionary process in itself and has taken several years. Previous versions of it were conceived with the input of Professors Gonzalo Zubieta, Sergio Vergara, and Ignacio Martín Maruri.

[21] John Naisbitt, *Global Paradox: The Bigger the World Economy, the More Powerful Its Smaller Players* (New York: William Morrow, 1994).

[22] This means that the chart in Figure 2-1 should be seen in a dynamic way. Since reality is always moving upward and to the right, the chart should reflect that. Otherwise, specific organizations will fall off the chart or type of organization to which it belongs.

23 This graph and Figures 2-5, 2-6, and 2-7 were developed in collaboration with Ignacio Martín Maruri.

24 Louis V. Gerstner Jr., *Who Says Elephants Can't Dance?* (New York: HarperCollins, 2002).

25 Other European telecommunications companies in Europe, such as France Telecom, Deutsche Telekom, British Telecom and Telecom Italia, followed a similar trend in those years as a result of industry liberalizationbut Telecom Italia and Telefonica clearly outperformed the rest.

26 Marco Celentani, "César Alierta," in *Testigos* (Madrid: FEDEA, 2011).

27 Fortune 500 ranking, 2013; see http://money.cnn.com/magazines/fortune/fortune500/.

28 The Forbes Global 2000, 2009; see http://www.forbes.com/lists/2009/18/global-09_The-Global-2000_Company_6.html. For the Forbes 1917 ranking and its evaluation in 1987, see Richard Foster and Sarah Kaplan, *Creative Destruction* (New York: Doubleday, 2001).

29 Richard N. Foster, *Creative Destruction Whips Through Corporate America* (Lexington, MA: Innosight, 2012).

30 See Frans De Waal, *Chimpanzee Politics: Power and Sex Among the Apes* (New York: Harper Colophon, 1982).

31 See Morton H. Fried, *The Notion of Tribe* (Menlo Park, CA: Cummings Publications, 1975).

32 Henry Ford applied the ideas of the American mechanical engineer Frederick W. Taylor, father of the discipline of scientific management. This was when the idea of productivity came into play, meaning that a worker should perform a task that would end up generating a product in the least possible time. Therefore, there had to be a few people designing the process, typically engineers, and a big bunch of workers executing the tasks that were considered in that design, without wasting any minute. Henry Ford's assembly line was the best materialization of these concepts, taking productivity to levels never seen before, which was followed by companies all over the place, generating a big step forward in the capacity of human beings for producing goods and, therefore, wealth.

33 Robert Slater, *Jack Welch and the GE Way* (New York: McGraw-Hill, 1999).

34 Organizations, as living systems, may also be thought of in terms of mechanical, organic, and social models. When related to adaptation, the first models

have the lowest adaptive capacity and the last ones have the highest. This has to do with how ingrained the idea of purpose is within the organization: in the mechanical model it is outside; in the organic model it is at the top; and in the social model it is distributed. See Jamshid Gharajedaghi and Russell L. Ackoff, "Mechanisms, Organisms and Social Systems," *Strategic Management Journal* 5/3 (July–September 1984): 289–300.

[35] *Hispanidad*, digital newspaper, November 4, 2013; see http://www. hispanidad.com/imagenes/CartaKey-4nov13.pdf.

[36] Telefonica's official website, news section, February 26, 2014; see http://pressoffice.telefonica.com/jsp/base.jsp?contenido=/jsp/ notasdeprensa/notadetalle.jsp&pagina=1&selectNumReg=5&id= 66&origen=resnotap&idm=eng&pais=1&elem=20613&mesinicio= 02&anioinicio=2014&mesfin=02&aniofin=2014&tlibre=.

[37] This widely used expression is a simplification of a more complex phrase written by Aristotle in his *Metaphysics*, Book 10, sec. 1045a: "What is the cause of the unification? In all things which have a plurality of parts, and which are not a total aggregate but a whole of some sort distinct from the parts, there is some cause." See Aristotle, *Metaphysics*, tran. Joe Sachs (Santa Fe, NM: Green Lion Press, 2002).

[38] Bill George, Diana Mayer, and Andrew N. McLean, *Andrea Young, Empowering Avon Women* (Boston: Harvard Business School Publishing, 2007).

[39] George Beham, *I, Steve: Steve Jobs in His Own Words* (Chicago: B2 Books, 2011).

[40] Walter Isaacson, *Steve Jobs* (New York: Simon & Schuster, 2011).

[41] For a deeper understanding of the importance of asking why, read Simon Sinek's *Start with Why: How Great Leaders Inspire Everyone to Take Action* (London: Penguin Books, 2009).

[42] Cited in Robert Kanigel, *The One Best Way: Frederick Winslow Taylor and the Enigma of Efficiency* (Cambridge, MA: MIT Press, 2005).

[43] For the full story and alternative explanations for Honda motorcycles' success in the United States, read "Perspectives on Strategy: The Real Story Behind Honda's Success," *California Management Review* (Spring 1984): 47–72.

[44] Amazon's 1997 Annual Report, available at the company's website: http://media.corporate-ir.net/media_files/irol/97/97664/reports/ Shareholderletter97.pdf.

[45] Noel M. Tichy and Stratford Sherman, *Control Your Destiny or Someone Else Will* (New York: Doubleday, 1993).

46 The case was documented by Jim Collins. For further reading, see his *Good to Great* (New York: HarperCollins, 2001).

47 William E. Fulmer, *Shaping the Adaptive Organization* (New York: AMACOM, 2000).

48 David Jackson, conversation with author, October 14, 2012.

49 The idea of boundaries providing a holding environment to creative work comes from Ronald Heifetz, in conversation with author, June 22, 2012.

50 *A Century of Innovation: The 3M Story* (St. Paul, MN: 3M Company, 2002).

51 Mary Jo Hatch with Ann L. Cunliff, *Organization Theory* (New York: Oxford University Press, 2006).

52 *Wall Street Journal*, February 9, 2011.

53 On how to use culture as a social control system, see Michael L. Tushman and Charles A. O'Reilly III, *Winning Through Innovation: A Practical Guide to Leading Organizational Change and Renewal* (Boston: Harvard Business School Publishing, 1997), chap. 5.

54 Thomas R. Eisenmann and Kerry Herman, *Google Inc.* (Boston: Harvard Business School Publishing, 2006).

55 To read more written from perspective of Google's employees, see Boris Groysberg, David A. Thomas and Alison Berkley Wagonfeld, *Keeping Google "Googley"* (Boston: Harvard Business School Publishing, 2008).

56 Starting from the impact of religion on social behavior, Max Weber wrote extensively about the relationship between culture and economic development. His 1905 *The Protestant Ethic and the Spirit of Capitalism* became a founding text in sociology (New York: Routledge, 2001).

57 Several authors, especially under the broader concept of social capital, have studied the impact of trust in social and economic development. See, for example, Robert D. Putnam, *Bowling Alone: The Collapse and Revival of American Community* (New York: Simon & Schuster, 2000); and Francis Fukuyama, *Trust: The Social Virtues and the Creation of Prosperity* (New York: Simon & Schuster, 1995).

58 The qualities of an adaptive culture have been the subject of reflection and development since the founding of Cambridge Leadership Associates, in 2002. A previous version of these qualities was outlined in Heifetz, Grashow, and Linsky, *The Practice of Adaptive Leadership*.

59 Groysberg, Thomas, and Wagonfeld, *Keeping Google "Googley."*

[60] The distinction between horizontal and vertical trust comes from Ronald Heifetz, in conversation with author, May 21, 2012.

[61] Jack Welch with John A. Byrne, *Jack: Straight from the Gut* (New York: Warner Books, 2001).

[62] *The American Heritage Dictionary of Indo-European Roots*, ed. Calvert Watkins, 2nd ed. (Boston: Houghton Mifflin Harcourt, 2000).

[63] Welch, *Jack: Straight from the Gut.*

[64] Bradford D. Smart, *Topgrading: How Leading Companies Win by Hiring, Coaching and Keeping the Best People* (New York: Penguin Group, 1999).

[65] Robert Safian, "This Is Generation Flux: Meet the Pioneers of the New (and Chaotic) Frontier of Business," *Fast Company*, January 9, 2012.

[66] Groysberg, Thomas, and Wagonfeld, *Keeping Google "Googley."*

[67] All quotes come from Reed Hastings, presentation to company employees, "Netflix Culture: Freedom and Responsibility," Los Gatos, California, August 1, 2009.

[68] Ibid.

[69] For a more comprehensive explanation of these tools, see Christopher A. Bartlett and Meg Wozny, *GE's Two-Decade Transformation: Jack Welch's Leadership* (Boston: Harvard Business School Publishing, 2005).

[70] Hastings, "Netflix Culture: Freedom and Responsibility."

[71] To know about how we lock up our potential and avoid change, see Robert Kegan and Lisa Laskow Lahey, *Immunity to Change: How to Overcome It and Unlock the Potential in Yourself and Your Organization* (Boston: Harvard Business School Publishing, 2009).

INDEX